EMBRACING THE JOURNEY: INSPIRING STORIES OF HOPE, HEALING, AND TRIUMPHING OVER ADVERSITY

Foreword by Dr. Kate Dow

Compiled by Kayla Brissi

Copyright

Embracing the Journey: Inspiring Stories of Hope, Healing, and Triumphing Over Adversity

ISBN: 978-1-7367397-1-6
Printed in the United States of America
First Printing: July, 2021
Publisher: Highly Favored Publishing LLC

Cover Design: Mariam Abid
Cover Image: Azaliya
Editing: Rebecca Camarena of Rebecca's Author Services

Dedication

To all those struggling and on the verge of giving up, may this anthology inspire you to embrace the journey you are on, find your inner warrior, transform your inner pain, and triumph over your adversity!

Acknowledgements

To my husband and son, thank you for your support, encouragement, and belief in me as an author. You are my motivation and inspiration behind everything I do. Love you!

To my friends and fellow co-authors of this anthology, I appreciate you more than words can say, and it is because of you, this book is in existence. Thank you for your bravery and willingness to share your story from an open heart about how you have triumphed over adversity. Your stories are an inspiration, and it has been an honor being on this journey with you.

To Dr. Kate Dow, thank you for your willingness to write the foreword for this book, sharing your insights and the profound work you do by supporting women to overcome their insecurities and overwhelm by utilizing their feminine wisdom and embodied empowerment.

To my editor, Rebecca Camarena, thank you for sharing your expertise and being part of my publishing team. Your guidance has helped improve our writing and allowed us to share our stories with passion and purpose.

To my family, friends, colleagues, mentors, and anyone else who has been a part of my life, whether it was for only a chapter or more, you've been an integral part of my journey and story; thank you.

EMBRACING THE JOURNEY: INSPIRING STORIES OF HOPE, HEALING, AND TRIUMPHING OVER ADVERSITY

Contents

Foreword 1

Introduction 7

Loving Myself: Learning to Live with PCOS.........................9
  Mindy Abbeduto

Answering the Call: Accepting My Divine Gifts 21
  Kayla Brissi

For Better or Worse: Caring for Your Spouse
with a Lifelong Illness and Disability................................35
  Rebecca Camarena

Beyond the Diagnosis: Thriving as a Special Needs Parent........44
  Lisa Ciao

A Lion's Roar: Transformation Through a Kundalini Awakening 50
  Tania Elena Gonzalez-Ortega

Grief and Loss: Hiding My Inner Pain After a Loved One's Death.....58
  Deborah Kos

The Beauty of Life: Surviving Tough Situations....................65
  Sonika Krüger

Body Confidence: Loving the Girl in the Mirror....................74
  Emma Jayne Lions

Darkness into Light: Breaking Free from Toxicity and Narcissism ... 84

    Sabita Saleem

Inner Transformation: Death Created Space for Growth 95

    Janine Shapiro

Empty Arms: Finding Joy After Loss 106

    Laura S. Shortridge

Moving Beyond the Inner Pain: Becoming Stronger,

Happier, and Healthier 115

    Dorota Soto

Anxiety Diary: A Journey to Self-Discovery 123

    Carrie Thompson

Transformation of Self: Turning Wounds into Wisdom

Through Healing My Identity 133

    Esmeralda Tridevi

Foreword

I'm Dr. Kate Dow, a psychologist, author, and spiritual coach, and I am so grateful to have been asked by Kayla Brissi to write a foreword for another one of her amazing books.

This profound book, *Embracing the Journey*, aligns beautifully with my own life experience and my work of Fear-less Feminine Wisdom that I teach to women worldwide. Each story reflects the courage, spirit and trust it takes to turn a life crisis into a soul awakening.

In her last powerful book in which she was a co-author *Out of My Comfort Zone: Stories of Courage, Perseverance and Victory* I was able to share about the fear and anxiety that women feel from stepping out of their comfort zone and how to best navigate it to help yourself feel more empowered, which I share in my book *Fear-Less: The Art of Using Anxiety to Your Advantage*.

Why does embracing the journey matter?

Life is challenging. How you meet life as consciously as you can, makes all the difference.

Fear of change is normal, and yet ongoing it can be debilitating.

It can block your confidence, and your sense of who you are, as you question whether you're in charge of your life.

For the most part you live your life being busy and focused on your daily routines, thinking you have got it all under control at some level.

And when things get uncomfortable or too challenging, you slowly start hiding and avoiding those tough parts. It's easier to stay in the comfort zone of what feels easier, better, and how we like it.

This works for a while.

And then life happens and a crisis hits.

You are forced to let go of your life as you like it. Your routine is gone. Everything has shifted and there is no going back. And you don't know what will happen next.

You are now in unknown territory. And it's changed everything.

It feels terrifying. How can you face the health issues, accidents, near death experiences, mental health crises, unbearable loss, career burnout, spiritual emergency...?

You lose your perspective as your world is turned upside down. You might even feel helpless, powerless, lost, forgotten, invisible, or worthless.

Like most people, you will go into crisis management mode and just handle it and believe you are unfazed. You maintain the facade that you have everything under control. And it temporarily detours you from the greater opportunity at hand.

It's OK, life will just bring you another one.

Eventually, there is the next crisis where nothing works. And it's like someone pulled the rug out from under you. All your coping strategies are failing. You can't deny the impact this time.

Now the disruption to your ordinary life has woken you up. You suddenly see the uncertainty you glossed over day to day, looming everywhere. It is frightening and beautiful all at once, because you suddenly can also see how very precious life is. Like it's under a magnifying glass.

This life disruption can feel like the worst thing that ever happened to you and yet where it takes you is the power of the journey.

And this is where the magic happens.

In these lucid moments, you pause and reflect within. You stop the running and turn around and face the fear, sadness, loss, and whatever else is present.

You dig deep and get courageous in your life. You begin to listen to your body, mind, and spirit. You feel all the emotion and stay present in your experience of what has happening.

You get real with yourself.
You get honest.
You find your brave.

And you begin to wake up.

And you suddenly see your life with fresh eyes and recognize where you were asleep, or missing in action, or sticking your head in the sand, or you were so busy you couldn't possibly feel how unhappy you were.

You begin to show up for yourself and become aware that this is your life and what are you going to do with it.

You begin to ask yourself things like "Where are you headed? Where do you want to go? and Who do you want to be?" You start revisiting the life you had before the crisis. You see clearly how playing small kept you stuck, unhappy and disempowered. You know now that you need to take full responsibility of yourself or nothing will change. But how?

"You can do it" an inner whisper speaks to you.

You don't know why but you just know this to be true. You simply take one step after the other, seeing your life: What has been, where you are, what you truly feel, what you have not said but need you, what you want to be different, where you need to be honest with yourself...

And despite being afraid, you begin to see the challenge, the crisis, or the devastation as the gift that it is.

The Gift of Facing What is

Facing our challenges, adversity and trauma are how we grow and evolve.

I learned of this ancient parable from a spiritual teacher. It is about this old farmer that is frustrated with God, because he cannot get a good crop. He tells God, "You may have created the world, but don't know the ABC's of farming. You have a lot to learn." God asks, "What is your advice?" And the farmer says "Give me a year's time and let everything be according to me and see what happens. Poverty will be gone."

God was willing to give him a year. And of course, the farmer asked for the best conditions, with no strong winds, no storms, and no dangers to the crops. Everything was perfect, easy, and best.

The wheat grew high, and the farmer was happy. The sun was out when he wanted sun, and rain came when he wanted it, in just the right amount. The farmer went and told God "Look how wonderful, these crops will be amazing for years, even if people don't work, there will be enough food."

But when the crops were harvested there was no wheat inside. The farmer was shocked and asked God "What happened? What went wrong?"

God said, "Because there were no difficulties, because there was no conflict or friction, because you avoided all that was "bad", the wheat remained impotent. A little struggle is necessary. Storms and lightning are needed. They are what shakes up the soul inside the wheat."

Just like the people, we want to be happy, but if we are happy all the time, it loses its meaning. We need sadness, loss to appreciate the happy times. Nighttime is as important as the day. When we stop trying to choose only what we want to experience and understand we need all kinds of life, we can appreciate the flow and natural rhythm of life and how it intelligently shakes our soul to grow.

When we look back on our lives, it is often the toughest parts that were the game changers, when we found hidden strengths, new desires, and directions, and became clearer about who we are and what matters to us most.

This is when we realize that our challenges are our gifts and can lead us to our best versions of ourselves. When we can accept life on life's terms, we can trust that whether it is a sunny or a stormy day, it is what we need to grow.

This trust is the magic of the feminine principles of receiving and allowing life to guide us. This helps balance with our masculine principles of acting and going after what we want. In harmony, they help us stay connected to ourselves and what is possible, no matter what is happening.

We know the challenges of the journey don't end, they just change, as we continue to grow, evolve, and embody more of our true nature.

We are learning to be less afraid to sit in the tough places and be open to change. We continue developing personally and spiritually and find those teachers, and mentors to guides us.

Then life becomes the journey of awakening.

Dr. Kate Dow
Author of Fear-Less: The Art of using Anxiety to Your Advantage
Psychologist-Spiritual Coach-Feminine Embodiment Guide
katedow.com

Introduction

"Embrace each challenge in your life as an opportunity for self-transformation." Bernie S. Siegel

One evening, during a powerful mindful meditation, ideas were swirling around in my head like the tornado from The Wizard of Oz, swooshing around, twisting, and turning until it all came to an abrupt stop. I knew beyond a shadow of a doubt what God was calling me to do. I received what I call a "Divine download," and the idea to publish an anthology was born!

The book you're about to read is unique and sure to leave an imprint on your heart and transform your life. The stories within the pages are incredibly inspiring and empowering. Each author shares their story bravely with passion and Divine purpose. Collectively they have come together with a similar mission in mind, to offer hope and healing to others on a similar journey.

The stories recount painful and even traumatic experiences in their life, and there's a little something for everyone. Topics include grief and loss of loved ones, miscarriages, divorce, mental health, or other health struggles, being a parent to a child with special needs and intellectual disabilities or becoming a full-time caregiver to the love of your life, and more!

In truth, when I read these stories, my heart swells, and I beam with pride over how far each author has come on their journey and the transformation that occurred.

We have women from various backgrounds, experiences, age groups, lifestyles, beliefs, even geographical locations, but they've come together as sisters to uplift and empower you to face your challenges with patience, perseverance, grit, and resilience.

No one is exempt from life challenges. These challenging circumstances force you to experience growth. When you boldly address the situation and take control over your life, magical things begin to happen. The stars align, and you find yourself on the other side with a new perspective. You might feel like you've been through hell and back, but you are stronger and wiser because of it!

On behalf of the co-authors, thank you for purchasing our book. May it empower you to find your inner strength, heal your inner pain, and triumph over the adversities of life.

With love and gratitude,

Kayla

Loving Myself: Learning to Live with PCOS

Mindy Abbeduto

As if being a teenager and becoming a woman wasn't hard enough as it was, I had to have crazy things going on within my body to make it even more awkward! My menstrual cycle was pretty irregular from onset but that isn't uncommon as a young teen, and doctors said that it can take up to a year for the body to become regular. I was also dealing with weight gain, especially in my mid-section, had spurts of acne and I started to experience excess hair, especially on my chin and upper lip. I remember my Mom asking me about my periods one day because I wasn't asking her to purchase pads or tampons. I lied to her and said I had a bunch from 'school' to use and that my cycle was light anyways. I wasn't very truthful about my cycle with her or any doctors actually. Pretended like everything was normal. I knew that something wasn't right, but secretly hoped it would eventually work itself out.

Turns out, I wasn't that lucky! My symptoms only got worse, of course since they weren't being treated. The weight was piling on despite how active I was. I had hair growing in places that shouldn't have grown, as a teenage girl and I felt so unattractive and alone. My self-esteem was non-existent, and I lacked confidence in every way possible. I was always heavier and would try to ignore comments from others about my weight. I desperately wanted to feel and look normal. I avoided playing sports, going to dances and doing many of the things other teenagers were doing. Wearing the clothes that were in style was usually out of the question as there wasn't much in the way of Plus size apparel at this time, so I had to either wear really 'mature' looking Plus size clothes or shop the men's section. I remember feeling so out of place!

I was applying for my first job after high-school and needed a pre-employment physical and some other tests done prior to being hired on. I was nervous to see a doctor for the first time in a long time, but also for the first time as an adult without having to have anyone else with me. I decided to be open and honest about the symptoms I was having surrounding my menstrual cycle, including the excess weight gain, unable to lose weight and the excess facial hair. The doctor I was seeing for the first time told me it sounded like it could be PCOS, but I was also obese and she "would not do any testing for PCOS until I lost a significant amount of weight", and that "when I lost the weight, my periods will balance themselves out." This was the first time I had heard the term polycystic ovarian syndrome (PCOS). PCOS is a condition that affects a woman's endocrine system and hormone levels. Women with PCOS produce higher-than-normal amounts of hormones, specifically androgens or male hormones in the body. This hormonal imbalance and high production of androgens prevent the ovaries from producing hormones and making eggs normally and causing cysts to form on the ovaries.

Now, I will admit I was heavier than I would have liked to have been and higher than the recommended range for my body type and age but I didn't think I was obese nor did I think that is what was causing the issues as I had them before I gained most of the excess weight. She didn't seem to want to listen when I was explaining to her that I exercised often and eat healthy or what I thought was healthy for me at the time but the weight kept creeping despite my efforts. It was as if she didn't believe me and I was wasting her time! I was pushed out the door with ways to lose weight and a brochure about obesity. Seriously? A brochure?! I felt mortified! And what was this PCOS stuff she was talking about?! I finally found the courage to talk to someone about what I was experiencing, and this is the response I got? It immediately closed me off. I didn't tell anyone about that appointment or what was going on within my body, at all! I secretly wished again that it would all work itself out.

As a young adult continuing to suffer from the same symptoms, dating or even going and doing normal things with friends was difficult because I had terrible social anxiety, I was still extremely uncomfortable in my body and would often get asked if I was expecting because of the excess weight in my belly area. On top of that, I certainly didn't want anyone to know my secret of having to pluck, wax and shave the excess hair on my body just to look and feel normal. At this point, I was trying everything possible to get rid of the embarrassing hair on my face that grew in better than most men's beards. I was having to shave every day or would attempt painful waxing or other hair removal techniques. Those attempts were always a temporary fix and would make me feel good in the moment, but it always came back.

I was always worried about my stubble showing towards the end of the day. With anything I did on a day-to-day basis, my facial hair was a concern, including things like getting a haircut, going to the dentist or the chiropractor, afraid that someone would notice and question me. I was shy, had no confidence and just kept to myself, always hiding the symptoms as best as I could with strict home beauty regimes, premium skincare, makeup and using shapewear, sometimes multiple shapewears under my clothing to hide what I felt was a misshapen and unattractive body shape I had acquired due to the hormonal weight I held. My weight and appearance were a constant battle for me.

I slowly began to gain my confidence while working in the beauty and fashion industry throughout my twenties at different jobs where I had access to everything I needed to look and feel pretty, along with working with some amazing groups of women. I began wanting to take better care of myself on the inside too and started exercising regularly again. Around this time is when the hype of the low-carb diets came to be popular and a few of us jumped on board and found great success! I was one of them! For the first time, I was seeing results. I was losing a lot of weight and inches while gaining confidence and my vibrant energy back. I felt good. People were raving about how much weight I had lost and how great I was looking. I felt like my PCOS symptoms were improving some. I still wasn't getting a regular cycle, but I was getting my period more often than I ever had in the past while skipping months. This was my normal for a long time.

A couple of years later when I moved into a new area and soon after entered a serious relationship. Wanting to be responsible, I knew that getting on birth control was my best bet since I dealt with an irregular period and there was no way of knowing when I was ovulating. I didn't want to worry about an unplanned pregnancy. I had to get established with a new doctor and was terrified! Thinking back to my horrible experience the last time I tried opening up to a doctor about my womanly issues. I set up an appointment with someone who specializes in women's health and felt at that point, I had nothing to lose and set out to obtain what I was going to get, which was birth control.

I was fortunate enough to have been seen by someone who had heard of PCOS and had treated patients with this condition. While it isn't certain what causes PCOS, this isn't a new condition and has been described amongst women's health records dating back to the early 1700's. She was confident that what I was experiencing was PCOS despite never actually being diagnosed. Remember, my last doctor wouldn't consider testing until I lost weight, so I never got an official diagnosis. My new doctor also said that testing for it was expensive and that insurance wouldn't cover most of it so before we tried any testing that I would have to pay out of pocket for, she got me set up on a medication, along with birth control specifically to help manage my symptoms and to regulate my period on top of contraception.

We ran a few minor tests to determine that yes, my hormones were all completely out of range, especially my androgen or male hormones and that I had high blood sugars which was causing insulin resistance and prompting the symptoms I was experiencing especially the irregular periods and hirsutism. Things were improving within a few weeks of my visit, the medications and the birth control were helping to regulate my cycle and eventually for the first time in my life, I was getting a regular period every month. Success!

I continued on my medications and birth control for a few years while also doing some research of my own on PCOS, what causes it, how to diagnose it, what symptoms were caused by it and really looking into what was going on inside my body. I started looking into the root causes of my symptoms. What was causing the high blood sugars and insulin resistance? How can I improve that? What was causing me to grow excess facial hair and how the hell do I rid that from even growing?! And what about all this excess weight in my tummy area no matter how much cardio, core and ab work I would do?? Am I going to look 5 months pregnant my entire life? I knew all of this was stemming from the hormonal imbalance, but I still didn't understand HOW it was causing these issues or the science behind it. There were still many symptoms that I was struggling with that I wanted answers to. Inflammation, Insulin Resistance and Genes have all been linked to excess androgen production which causes a plethora of issues within the body such as infertility, diabetes, obesity, endometrial cancer, depression, anxiety, metabolic syndrome, sleep apnea and along with it, an array of symptoms like irregular menstrual cycles, hair growth or hirsutism, hair loss, acne, weight gain, heavy bleeding, headaches and mental health issues. This condition affects up to 27% of women during childbearing years of age.

I pressed my doctors to start the testing for PCOS, looking into what my insurance at the time would cover, which wasn't much but I wanted to know more about what was going on INSIDE my body and requested blood work and a hormone panel test, so I knew where my levels were at. With my own research, I learned that to improve insulin resistance or insulin sensitivity, it was recommended to follow a low carb diet and to also reduce dairy and gluten. Getting a diagnosis was difficult! It has been becoming more of a topic amongst women's health more so over the last 20 years and the medical community is doing more research, learning more about ways to treat it and finding that it is becoming more common with women today. No wonder I had such great success following that style of eating in the past! Over the years, I followed that recommendation as much as possible but would go in spurts where my diet and nutrition got a little out of control, my weight would creep up rapidly and take twice as long to try and shed. Vicious cycle, it was. I was always quite active and into fitness. I played around with running, weightlifting, HIIT style workouts but just mainly looked to stay active. I found that if I was consistent with my efforts of eating the right foods and exercising, I could maintain my weight and maybe drop a couple pounds here and there, even if it was only temporary.

As I was nearing my forties, with my hormones changing, my cycles were beginning to change and my periods were getting worse. Heavier, longer, darker, excessive clotting, pain, headaches, cramps, and menstrual symptoms I had never experienced before. Each month got worse. I had sent a note to my doctor to ask if I should be concerned and it was chalked up to my hormones changing and as I get older, and that my periods may not always look the same. It sounded logical but I wasn't convinced. I was always reading articles and books about PCOS, trying to learn more. One day, I came across a conversation in a forum that was discussing the dangers of being on birth control for an excess period of time and was describing much of what I was experiencing.

I did more research and found much of the same information, especially with women who were previously diagnosed with PCOS and given birth control to help regulate their cycles. When on birth control, your body has a period prompted by the additional hormones in the birth control. It isn't considered a true period where your body would go through that shedding naturally. I knew my body wasn't menstruating on its own and it was only functioning because of the hormones in the birth control. All of that on top of how much my cycle had changed over time, it started to make sense to me and I soon began to realize that the birth control and medication I was on was really only a "band-aid" for my PCOS symptoms. I remember thinking to myself, 'How is this any different from when I wasn't ovulating and menstruating on my own? My body still isn't functioning properly!"

At the time, I felt completely out of control with my body, my career was stressing me out, my hormones were crazy out of control and I was experiencing major mood swings, anxiety, depression, low libido, brain fog, insomnia and had zero energy for anything. My weight was up, and I was dealing with a lot of inflammation. My stress was worsening and cortisol levels were rising, causing my anxiety and depression to deepen. This was affecting not only my day-to-day life, but my marriage and even my job. I eventually was put on anxiety medication, and it was suggested that I try other methods to healing as well, such as doing yoga and possibly therapy to help work through emotions and reduce stress.

All of this was being caused by the effects of being on birth control long term and my hormonal and endocrine system being very unbalanced. I knew something had to change and made the decision, with my doctor's approval, to wean my body off all medications and birth control to help reset my system.

I had been following a few people in the online space whose passions included women's health, hormonal imbalances and tackling PCOS at its core by addressing the issues at their root cause. With me, based on the testing I had requested with my doctor I knew that I needed to lower my androgen hormones, improve insulin resistance, and lower my cortisol (stress) levels. These were the three hormones that were most out of balance for me consistently and what I wanted to address.

At the time, I felt miserable. Miserable inside my body and how I looked on the outside. Puffy and unattractive. Despite those feelings, I also had hope and was eager to try and tackle my PCOS symptoms and the havoc it was wreaking on my body through alternative forms of healing and a holistic and nutritional approach. I immediately got to work!

Lowering stress was the easiest for me to tackle solo while I continued to work through a couple holistic programs, learning about improving insulin resistance through a nutritional standpoint. For my diet and nutrition, I knew that following a low-carb diet, reducing dairy and gluten was going to help reduce the amount of sugars and carbohydrates going into my system and improve my insulin sensitivity. With insulin resistance, my body doesn't respond to insulin as it should nor does it process carbohydrates like a normal healthy body would. It can't convert that food into energy for the body to burn and instead stores it as fat, which contributes to the weight gain. Getting consistent with my eating habits was key for me. I also started taking supplements and drinking herbal teas made specifically for women with hormonal disorders and PCOS.

Movement was also important for me to keep my energy levels up and to help burn stored fat. I did a lot of HIIT style working out, walking, and I enjoyed taking hikes in the woods as it was therapeutic for me. I started doing a lot of yoga, including meditating and deep breathing techniques to help with my stress and anxiety. When I went off my birth control, I began tracking my cycles and keeping a food log so that I had something to go off of and see how my body was responding to the things I was doing over time. I had read that it may take a while for my cycle to adjust after stopping BC and that it was possible that my body wouldn't ovulate, much like how it was years ago when I had irregular and absent periods.

Imagine my surprise when my first cycle came just 45 days after going off the medication! I couldn't believe it! What I also couldn't believe was that it was a completely different period than the painful, traumatic ones I was experiencing that year leading up to when I decided to go off the pill. For the first time in a long time, my period appeared and felt normal. There was no painful cramping or bloating. I remember thinking to myself, 'This is just a fluke!' but encouraged myself to keep up with my efforts.

Over time, with being consistent with eating the right foods for my body, which happen to be low-carbohydrate based, low-dairy, no processed foods, no gluten and staying active and staying balanced, my PCOS symptoms were improving. I was losing weight slowly, my energy levels were being restored, I was noticing less hair growing in on my face and neck area. The more consistent I was with my efforts, the more regular my cycle became and the shorter it was in length. I am proud to say that I have had a 36-day average cycle for nearly three years now without the assistance from artificial hormones, medication, or surgeries.

My hormones are still unbalanced but they are becoming closer in range of where they should be. I still struggle with my weight but I no longer beat myself up over it knowing it's harder for someone with my condition to lose weight. I still have to deal with facial hair on a daily basis and sometimes carry a fresh razor with me in case I need a touch up during the day but it is improving. I still struggle to get a consistent amount of sleep. Insomnia is something that many ladies with PCOS deal with. My inflammation has improved. Through all of this, I have been also trying to reduce the amount of chemicals and toxins entering my body by eliminating the use of makeup, skincare products, hair dye, the use of cleaning products at home and taking measures to keep the air in my home and work clean and filtered.

Nearly everything I do on a daily basis is done to support my PCOS and hormone balancing from planning out my meals, counting carbs and macros, logging what I eat, ensuring I'm eating enough and often enough so my blood sugar remains stable and it's not having to produce excess insulin that my body doesn't recognize that could lead to Type 2 Diabetes; making sure to take my supplements and drink the teas that support healthy hormone function; getting enough exercise to boost my energy and burn fat, but not overdoing it because that is taxing on my body, raising cortisol levels (which is a hormone!); getting enough quality sleep; lowering stress and anxiety and so on.

Taking care of my body inside and out has become a passion of mine and I am fascinated about what I've learned about my body over the years. I enjoy reading new articles and hearing about what other Doctors and medical professionals are finding with PCOS now. I spend a lot of time talking with other women about PCOS and our symptoms in groups I'm in and a part of and it's amazing what each person's unique experience is yet we can still support one another and learn new things from each other. I'm always learning!

I am a huge advocate of self-care and have found support through my yoga practice to help keep me feeling balanced in my body, to help control my emotions and support my anxiety. Mindful living and managing my PCOS on a more holistic approach has helped me become more in tune with my body and have that awareness of what it is going through and struggling with while having this condition.

My dream one day is to help other women struggling with polycystic ovarian syndrome understand everything about it and to help empower them to take control over their condition and symptoms with confidence.

Mindy Abbeduto is the proud owner of Minderella Designs & Events and Alluring Artistry LLC, a Women's Health Advocate, and co-author of *Embracing the Journey: Inspiring Stories of Hope, Healing and Triumphing over Adversity*.

She has been a thriving entrepreneur for over eight years, bringing her creativity and attention to detail to both the wedding and beauty industry through her two businesses.

As a wedding planner, designer, and florist, Mindy has assisted numerous couples through the wedding planning process and helped turn their wedding dreams into reality.

Minderella Designs & Events is listed and featured as a preferred vendor with The Wedding Planner and Guide, a local source for Southern Wisconsin's couples. Mindy also has a wedding blog, been featured in online magazines, and has written articles for the local Hometown News' and other wedding-related publications.

With her other business, Alluring Artistry LLC, she brings her skills into the beauty industry offering specialty beauty services as a certified Eyelash Extension technician and a certified Permanent Makeup Artist, offering cosmetic tattooing and permanent makeup services. She has recently become an assistant trainer with Advanced Permanent Cosmetic Academy in Middleton, WI, where Mindy has received her education and advanced training and holds three certifications in permanent makeup advanced techniques.

In addition to yoga and cooking, Mindy enjoys having theme parties and hosting friends and family. Being in nature is where she finds peace and enjoys outdoor excursions with her husband Ryan and two dogs, Gus and Duke.

With her busy work life, Mindy believes in obtaining work and life balance and is an advocate for self-care and mindful living.

To learn more about Mindy, please follow her online at facebook.com/mindyabbedutoauthor.

Answering the Call: Accepting My Divine Gifts

Kayla Brissi

As a child, nature always drew me in like a moth to a flame. I loved being at our family camp in Stonington, Michigan, where I could roam free. The pristine beach with clear waters was just a short walk from our lot. I remember getting lost in thought, looking up at the beautiful green leaves overhead, listening to the wildlife around me, the gravel crumbling under my shoes, and the waves crashing in the distance. I was at peace and in my element.

I used to scour the shoreline, looking for fossils or other remarkable looking rocks, driftwood, and beach glass. Sometimes I would have so many treasures that I struggled to carry them back to where my parents were sitting and had to make the painful decision to leave some behind.

There are numerous stories of my childhood about being in nature, from accompanying my dad when he would hunt to us fishing together, going canoeing, and more. Each one unique in its own right, but what I can tell you is nature recharges my proverbial batteries, and it has always been a place where I could let go, tune inward, and connect with God.

I grew up as a cradle Catholic, and at an early age, became quite devout. I could recite prayers my peers couldn't. I eagerly completed my sacraments, and I loved going to church! In short, it was a profound spiritual connection, or so I thought.

In my early teens, I realized that I struggled to pray the way I once did and discovered that having "daily conversations" with God was what felt aligned to me. We would talk wherever and whenever, and it quickly evolved into a relationship much like two best friends who couldn't wait to speak to each other and share their secrets and dish about the latest gossip.

I always had a special bond with my dad, almost as if a deeper Divine reason was at play, and I quickly realized that I needed to get involved in things he enjoyed if I wanted to be around him more. Therefore, I learned how to hunt and fish and everything I could about canoeing. I showed interest in anything he wanted to show me. Whether it was learning about coins, practicing fly fishing, or woodworking, I soaked it up like a sponge. Truthfully, I didn't care what we did together; I just wanted to tag along like his shadow and be in his presence.

Time with my dad, in nature, always felt like home. And in these moments, it was when I often connected with God and shared my innermost secrets, thoughts, and prayers privately. As a result, nature became part of my worldly church, a place to connect with the Divine, deepen the relationship, and be myself unapologetically.

Throughout the years, I eventually found my way back to the church and, at one point, believed it was the only place I could be a devout Christian. The symbolism of the church, the programming from my childhood, and encouragement from loved ones led me back. At the time, I was content. It seemed to be what I needed during that chapter of my life.

Shortly after my dad transitioned and was called home to be with our Lord, I experienced a turbulent time in my life. I struggled to control my emotions, became highly reactive, and later was diagnosed with severe depression, generalized anxiety disorder (GAD), and indications of post-traumatic stress disorder (PTSD).

In a nutshell, the foundation of my life crumbled. I felt like a complete failure and was embarrassed that I, the strong one of the family, was now weak, or so I thought. However, I graciously accepted the help of a medical professional to get my life back on track because I knew I needed to pick up the pieces of my life since my son, husband, family, and clients were counting on me for various things.

Interestingly, within the breakdown, despite feeling broken emotionally, mentally, physically, and spiritually, things within and around me began to shift.

After my dad's passing, regretfully, my relationship with God became quite strained. Going to church became a trigger for me emotionally, mentally, physically, and spiritually. It became too much to bear. I eventually decided that enough was enough.

I accepted that going to church wouldn't be part of my plan for now during this phase of my life. With that, I embraced the worldly church I once was fond of and opened myself up to the idea that I could still practice my religious beliefs and connect with God outside the church. I let go of the programming of how a Catholic should practice the religion and accepted a spiritual practice that felt aligned for me; it felt like home.

Truthfully, I held strong onto my faith throughout his treatment, prayed fervently, asked for healing, and felt that God didn't answer my prayers. If I'm completely honest with myself, I was angry! I needed someone to blame for his death. I blamed Him, the US Government for his Agent Orange exposure during Vietnam, and myself.

Yes, I blamed myself.

As I continually replay the last year of his life, I often think about the 'what ifs' and wonder if I had made the right choices. Did I say everything I needed to say to him? That's the challenging part about grief and loss and coping with a mental illness. Living in constant wonder of 'what ifs' worrying about things that are no longer in your control, and not like they were, to begin with, either.

I cannot change the past, but I can learn from it. I can use it to fuel the fire burning within and allow all the pain to serve a greater purpose. That purpose became abundantly clear after I finally told my ego to take a damn seat, and I surrendered.

My life began to change when God aligned the stars for my mom and me to attend a Mind, Body, Spirit Fair. My mom expressed interest in attending a group reading with a Medium in hopes of receiving a message from my late father. Admittedly, I was skeptical and afraid. However, I didn't want my mother to go alone; so I reluctantly and curiously accompanied her. Armed with my rosary in my pocket and a cross necklace hidden under my clothes, I was spiritually prepared.

And that's the ironic thing about all of this. I have always believed in angels, ghosts, spirits, and life after death. The notion that we die and that's it never sat well with me. It's as if I always knew there was more to death and dying. So why was I afraid now or acting as if none of it were real? Conditioning from the church, society, friends, family? Fear, perhaps. All of the above? Most likely.

As I sat across the room from the Medium, looking around the circle of loved ones eagerly waiting for a message, I studied her, trying to gauge her authenticity. My stomach was churning and feeling in knots, but I curiously watched and listened to her deliver messages of love, hope, and inspiration to strangers. Messages from beyond the grave, from heaven, and even though she delivered heartfelt messages with astounding accuracy for others, I still felt a bit skeptical. However, I remained hopeful that I would receive a message too.

I was lost in the wonder of the moment and quickly came to when my eyes locked hers, and she completely caught me off guard with the message she provided me. Chills occurred all over my body, and I instantly burst into tears. I cried like a baby in front of my mother and a room full of strangers. Talk about embarrassing!

I knew beyond a shadow of a doubt that this message came from my dad. There is absolutely no way she could have known what she did. She couldn't have done any research about my loved ones or me either. There's no denying she was the real deal!

My journey to healing from my grief started soon after that experience. Meeting this Medium, I believe, was Divine intervention. God placed her in my life at the exact moment I needed her.

The beautiful moment we shared as she delivered a message from my dad was beyond what I ever thought possible, and it opened my heart and the doors to my healing journey and the spiritual world. I cannot deny what I have personally experienced and witnessed. They say seeing is believing, and I 100% believe that!

Months later, I connected with another believer, a Psychic Medium to be exact, and they kicked open the spiritual door more fully. It was then that I began to experience unexplainable things myself.

As a suggestion, I was encouraged to write in my journal to my dad to see if he would communicate. Honestly, I didn't know what I was doing or if it would even work, but I decided to give it a try. At this point, what did I have to lose?

After saying a prayer, asking for protection, and getting into a meditative state, I ask in my head, "Dad are you there? Can you give me a sign?" I felt foolish, but I was committed to the process, so I patiently waited for a sign or anything at all that would indicate he was with me in spirit.

There I sat sprawled out on the love seat with my head resting in my hand on the arm of the couch, thinking I legit must be crazy or extremely desperate when suddenly, I distinctly felt a shove at the lower part of my back.

Thinking it's just a coincidence but wanting confirmation, I internally asked, "Dad, if that was you, please do it again." A few seconds later, I felt a shove on my wrist with such force; it kicked it out from beneath my head, causing it to drop onto the arm of the couch. I sat there in utter disbelief. Wondering, how could this even be possible?

Thoroughly intrigued, I internally asked for the third time for him to prove that it was him. I guess you could say I was testing him. Well, I got my sign! Within seconds I felt hard shoves on my upper back, right wrist twice, my lower back, and legs as if he was poking at me playfully.

Frazzled, I sat straight up with chills running up and down my body. I tried to find a logical explanation, like I dozed off and my head dipped or that it was a muscle spasm; however, I knew in my heart there was only one explanation no matter how crazy it may seem, it was my dad.

With each playful shove, the movement felt as they did growing up. As kids, my dad would give us a little push when goofing around with us girls. There was no denying it was him, and I knew we were communicating beyond a shadow of a doubt. He was there with me.

After confirmation that he was with me, I wrote a question down in my journal for him. I closed my eyes, got back into a meditative state, and tuned into any messages that may come through. My goal was to notice what I noticed; that's it.

The most significant sign I received was as if a movie was playing in my mind's eye, and as I watched it play before me, the answer to my

26

question came through. The attention to detail, vibrant colors, and, I'll say, storyline since it was similar to a movie, were impressive. Simply amazing!

I was later encouraged to read tarot cards by the Psychic Medium, who insisted I knew how to read them—not believing that I had any such spiritual gifts, I gave it a whirl. Unbeknownst to me, I did possess such a gift! I seemed to know things without knowing how I knew them and delivered accurate readings to strangers that provided specific details about their lives. As a collective, we were all astonished! How is this real?

Over the coming months, I continued to practice using my gifts and deepening my understanding of the spiritual world privately. I had to learn a difficult lesson about discernment and to listen to my intuition fully. Unfortunately, that lesson taught me that some people are masquerading around and claim to be of "love and light" when in reality, they're not.

This hard truth cost me nearly everything I worked hard to build: my marriage, personal and professional relationships, my businesses, and more. It sucked, and I spent a significant amount of time repairing and rebuilding what I nearly lost. This experience has led me to become increasingly selective with whom I choose to do work with and has significantly helped in this spiritual journey. It also taught me to be more careful about the proverbial doors I was opening too!

For nearly two years, I kept my spiritual gifts a secret and only shared them with people I knew I could trust. It isn't exactly the information you want just anyone to have.

Coming from a Christian upbringing and the shame and stigmas around people with spiritual gifts such as being a Psychic Medium or a healer were often seen as work of the devil, ungodly, or un-Christian-like. I was afraid of what my family, friends, colleagues, and clients who identified as Christian would think of my gifts. Would they accept them or disown me?

Having been diagnosed with a mental illness, I feared this information would land in the wrong ears, and others would see me as "crazy" or that someone would try to take my son away from me. I worried about how my devout Catholic husband would react to my gifts and whether it would put further strain on our marriage.

While I am beyond grateful for these gifts that God bestowed upon me, I would be remiss if I didn't admit the inner turmoil I experienced and the plaguing fear of what would happen if this information wasn't well received.

Regrettably, at times, this fear stifled my gifts. I wrestled internally for a long time about whether I should embrace what gifts I received or bury them down deep within like I often do with most things that create uncomfortable and anxiety-ridden experiences.

One day I decided I needed answers and wanted them now. The inner turmoil, the secrets, feeling as though I was lying to my loved ones, was eating me alive! I felt two-faced and like a fraud.

How can I claim to be a Christian and be interested in the "woo-woo" or spiritual realm? Don't they contradict each other? So many conflicting thoughts were racing through my head for a long time on repeat, which became mentally, emotionally, and spiritually exhausting!

On the one hand, I felt that my Christian upbringing, the beliefs instilled upon me, the deep shame and guilt that I was experiencing led me to believe that I would let so many people down. I feared their wrath of judgment and ridicule. I was afraid to be kicked out of the church and to be ostracized, which of course, I know is absurd, but I'm also a realist and know anything is possible.

I have come to understand that people fear what they don't know or completely understand, and I know this topic is one that many conservative Christians often fear. Heck, I was one of them!

Unfortunately, I have lost some friends, business partnerships, and clients because of this journey. I was even kicked out of an international "club" per say for Christian business owners as a founding member because I no longer met their standards as a Christian. Truthfully, I wasn't in the slightest surprised when I received the private message when mere weeks before, a yoga practitioner got the boot because that too didn't fit their skewed perception of being a Christian. I knew my days were numbered and made peace with it.

Did it sting a bit not to be accepted for being me? Yes, of course, it did, but not nearly as bad as what I believed it could be. I may have gotten bruised from the experience, but I will live—just another lesson I had to learn and another chapter in the book of my life.

However, on the other hand, it felt wrong for me to deny these spiritual gifts. I didn't ask for them; I guess you could say I was born with them. However, it seems the traumatic passing of my dad blew open the door to this awakening, and what I have briefly shared doesn't even scratch the surface of my spiritual abilities.

I pondered about the existence of these gifts. I questioned myself and wondered that if they truly came from God and were used for Godly reasons, how could they possibly be the devil's work? Being rather inquisitive, I embarked on a journey to find the truth. I questioned everything! My Christian beliefs, morals and values, the purpose of these gifts, and so much more.

What I discovered was me and who I am at my core. I shed layers of my being, like an onion, and began to see the bigger picture. Fear dissipated, and I stepped more into my inner power, my authentic truth.

I rediscovered myself, found my inner spiritual warrior, and explored my higher calling. One in which I would embrace the gifts bestowed upon me to help others. I learned to transmute the pain into my purpose!

It's no coincidence that within the first year of my dad's passing, I had around seven clients lose a parent, and before the two-year mark, I supported three more with the loss of a dear loved one.

Working with grief and loss, trauma, mental health diagnoses, and more while building a business became part of my coaching practice. Supporting my clients in their healing journey was part of my higher calling, and it allowed me to create a framework to help others in this journey.

One day I had an epiphany. As much as I wish my dad were still here with us, I know now that I had to experience the deep inner pain and traumatic experience to embrace and step into my Divine purpose. I don't believe in coincidences; I genuinely believe that everything happens for a reason even if I don't fully understand at the time, hindsight is always 20/20, and the answers always reveal themselves over time.

Interestingly, in communicating with spiritual mentors, we discussed losing my dad, and the turmoil I experienced was all part of my soul's contract for this Earthly experience. That unique bond I mentioned that I had with my father, well, I was informed that we are part of the same soul family and our souls' had a contract with each other. Admittedly, this spiritual philosophy was a bit "out there" for me at the time, but when you remove the ego, judgmental thoughts, and fear, it makes sense in the grand scheme of things.

I realized that I was not ready years ago to accept this calling. My blinders were on, and I could not see the greater vision and plan God had for my life. My ego was too much in control, and I needed to humble myself by having my life burn to the ground so I could rise from the ashes like a phoenix, renewed and transformed.

So while I still support my clients as a business coach and marketing strategist, I have fully accepted the path of being a life coach and holistic healing practitioner. I embrace my spiritual gifts and utilize them within my practice.

The work I do is profound, and there's a Divine purpose for it, no doubt.

When I think about the work I do, there are so many facets to it, and it can be complicated to explain it at times succinctly. However, it's with great pleasure that I can share that I learned how to embrace the journey, transform my inner pain, and reclaim my life.

It's a blessing to guide my clients to break free from limiting beliefs and stuck patterns by helping them unleash their inner warrior so they can regain control over their lives and live with more passion and purpose.

Part of my mission is to transcend limits, break barriers, and transform lives globally by no longer hiding behind fear and standing in my authentic truth!

With that said, let me leave you with this one final piece of unsolicited advice; if you identify as a Christian, stop with the judgment and open your heart and mind. Love and accept one another. Be kind.

Someone wise once said, "God doesn't call the qualified, but he qualifies the called," and I wholeheartedly believe that!

James 1:16-18 says, "Don't be deceived, my dear brothers and sisters. Every good and perfect gift is from above, coming down from the Father of the heavenly lights, who does not change like shifting shadows. He chose to give us birth through the word of truth, that we might be a kind of first fruits of all he created."

Therefore, if you're like me, I want to encourage you to honor and embrace your Divine gifts and do your Godly work!

Kayla Brissi is a multi-passionate entrepreneur, speaker, author, and the owner of Kayla Brissi LLC and Intuitive Spiritual Warrior Holistic Consulting & Healing LLC.

As a life transformation strategist, Kayla guides her clients to break free from limiting beliefs and stuck patterns by helping them unleash their inner warrior so they can regain control over their lives and live with more passion and purpose.

Her mission is to transcend limits, break barriers, and transform lives globally!

Kayla has contributed to numerous industry publications and online platforms such as Thrive Global, Today, and Skillshare. In addition, FOX, NBC, CBS, MarketWatch, Digital Journal, and various other sites and digital magazines have featured Kayla, and multiple podcasts and radio shows have interviewed her over the years.

She is also the author of *Healing from Grief: Transform Your Pain Into Purpose and Honor Your Loved One* and *Transforming Inner Pain: Moving Beyond the Grief and Reclaiming Your Life After Loss* and the co-author of various anthologies: *The Beauty in My Mess: Stories of Truth, Transparencies and Triumphs, Driven: A Guidebook for Women by Women; To Inspire and Empower, Out of My Comfort Zone: Stories of Courage, Perseverance and Victory, Dust to Salvation: Stories of Grace, Love, and Redemption in the Midst of Jesus Revealing Unexpected Miracles*, and *Embracing the Journey: Inspiring Stories of Hope, Healing and Triumphing over Adversity*.

Kayla has a Masters in Business Administration with a concentration in finance and a Bachelor of Arts degree in both Accounting and Business Administration from Lakeland University (formerly Lakeland College) and a Financial Services Technical Diploma from Mid-State Technical College.

She has also acquired various coaching, holistic healing, and spiritual certifications that have allowed her to provide unparalleled support for her clients regarding their life transformation.

When Kayla's not writing her next best-selling book or helping her clients bulldoze through the proverbial locked doors, you can catch her eating ice cream, reading a book or watching a movie, and spending time with her family.

To learn more about Kayla, please visit her website at kaylabrissi.com.

For Better or Worse: Caring for Your Spouse with a Lifelong Illness and Disability

Rebecca Camarena

All had seemed well at our Friday night dinner. A few hours that let us unwind from the pressure of the week. It was a simple dinner at one of our favorite restaurants. Could you have seen us had you been in the restaurant, you would have seen how utterly unprepared we were for our life to be turned upside down.

In her book, *The Year of Magical Thinking*, Joan Didion states that Life changes fast. Life changes in an Instant. You sit down to dinner and life as you know it ends.

And the next morning my husband didn't feel good.

He stayed home and went to urgent care while my daughter and I went to the annual Los Angeles Times Book Festival. This was a feat in itself maneuvering through L.A. traffic. It was the first of many things that I would do by myself that we normally did together.

In a matter of days a simple infection sent him to the hospital and he was diagnosed with sepsis. In the coming weeks, months, and years my husband would at times fight for his life and go through one hospitalization after another, numerous surgeries, some emergency and some planned, and more to repair the damage caused by Osteomyelitis in the spine.

Amidst the chaos and the shocking health news the doctor explained the results of what she was going to do in this first emergency surgery in July 2019. It was only three months after the hospital declared him free of sepsis. It was too much to understand. I was powerless to grasp what was happening. *I wondered how an infection can destroy bone so quickly.* We both thought it was only a slipped disc in his back.

In his room the beeping of the machines was the only sound. He was asleep with the IV lines pumping antibiotics and other drugs to help rid his body of infection, it hurt me deeply watching him lie in the bed. Had this been anyone else at the hospital he would have wrapped his arms around me and I would lay my head on his shoulder, he was that much taller than me. I leaned against the wall for support, a poor substitute for his warm shoulder. It was ironic that as I watched the fireworks out the third floor window as the nation celebrated Independence Day we were losing our independence.

I grew up with the romantic narrative of the Disney fairy tales of the late 60's and early 70's, the ones with Prince Charming marrying the love of his life, making her a Princess and they would live happily ever after but no one ever revealed what went on after the end of the film.

I never imagined my fairytale would turn out like this.

My husband and I grew up with the narrative that hard work would get us what we wanted. We plowed through life with a determination to do, to achieve, to accomplish. We raised children, bought a house and provided for our children. However, we failed to plan for being sick. We took our health for granted. Things which only happened to other people were in fact happening to us. Our marriage vows, for better or worse, didn't define how much worse things would become.

This was never supposed to happen to him; to us.

He left the hospital to spend the summer in a "skilled nursing facility" receiving daily IV antibiotics and learning to walk with a weakened spine missing three lower discs in his back.

During this summer I appeared on the face of it, a competent person. I helped clients see their dreams come true and become published authors. I launched my women's anthology book *Out of My Comfort Zone: Stories of Courage, Perseverance and Victory*. I became an international best-selling author while I sat next to his bed.

This was not the narrative I imagined when I became an author.

I was responsible. I paid bills, ran the house, stressed about the paranoia of the time, provided daycare for my granddaughter's, renewed my driver's license, got a smog check on my car and took care of getting the car repaired after an accident along with overseeing a number of major home improvements.

With the same determination that he approached everything else he was going to go back to work. Then the doctor dropped a bombshell and said he wouldn't be able to go back to work. His back would never be as strong as it was and he needed lots of physical therapy. She advised him to retire. RETIREMENT? *We weren't ready for it.* Retirement was on the horizon and years away. Old people retired. *We weren't old enough or rich enough to retire.*

I couldn't imagine that our life as we knew it was over. We had spent our entire life always being active and on the go. The freedoms we had to be spontaneous to get in a car and go for a day trip, our family camping trips, walks on the beach and around our neighborhood. I mourned our old life - the ease at which we enjoyed life - our individual independence and our collective independence.

The sadness of our situation weighed on me heavily. I had to accept the fact that our life had changed. Our roles had changed, he always provided and took care of me. But, now his needs were and would always be greater than mine.

Some days it was mind numbing and overwhelming. My emotions went from sad, exhausted, grieving and worried. When I opened my eyes each morning the reality hit me that our life was changed. I had lost my spark. I felt I was slowly fading away. I grieved our old life. I grieved the memories of the good times. I couldn't get past it. My world had been shaken and ripped apart.

I had the hardest job of my life handed to me being his caregiver each time he came home from the hospital. The work of a caregiver 24/7 went from not only tending to my husband's needs but coordinating home health care appointments, appealing incorrectly charged medical bills, and navigating mountains of paperwork for early retirement. I was doing skilled nursing tasks - administering IV medicines daily for a period of time.

I never wanted to be a nurse even though most everyone in my family was in the medical field. I was a rebel, always wanting to be a writer and an author. I was fine when home health care nursing was with us but when they discharged him yet he still wasn't quite well enough to care for himself I panicked and wondered, *how I would do it all.*

There is no step-by-step manual for either patient or caregiver and illness and injury; each person is different. It takes courage, perseverance and patience for both the patient and caregiver. This wasn't an illness that was going to be gone in six weeks like a broken arm.

How was I to keep going when even the simplest tasks seemed monumental?

I was overwhelmed and tired, more tired than I ever could imagine. I was in pain; physical pain, emotional pain and mental pain. I deferred my health to another day, another time and ended up nursing one injury after another: pulled muscles, ankle pain and then I fell hard and injured my knees. I spent the next few weeks with ice wrapped around my knees. How did I work through the pain? The physical would heal eventually but I was fighting a war inside my head every single day rebelling against the life we were living mostly in the hospital.

In 2020 the year of the pandemic he spent more than five weeks undergoing another major surgery and recovery in the acute rehab unit within the hospital. No visitors were allowed because of the Coronavirus restrictions. I could see the hospital, could walk to it, but couldn't get in to see him. Not having been separated from each other for more than a week at a time it was hard to accept this "no visitors allowed" policy. I couldn't control what was happening with his health so once again *I was responsible* and set up a GoFundMe Campaign to raise money to pay for our mounting medical bills.

And when he was released and came home he was unable to walk from his last spine surgery. The doctor said time would tell if the nerves in his spine would heal and he MIGHT walk again. And he was so sick. Each time he underwent surgery it took his body that much longer to heal.

This was never supposed to happen to him; to us.

I longed for our old carefree lifestyle. I replayed memories over and over in my head of happier days of our carefree days and life as we knew it. I wondered how we were going to get through this. *How did things go so wrong? How much more could we handle? How much more could I handle?*

There were times when I wondered if we'd ever have anything that resembled a normal life. Even though I didn't know what normal would look like if he couldn't walk now and might not walk. There were times that I didn't believe I could get through it. I came across another quote. I don't know who said it, but it was meant for me. "Courage doesn't always roar. Sometimes courage is the little voice at the end of the day that says, "I'll try again tomorrow.'"

I had to celebrate my strength and find my courage to go on.

I kept it all inside of me and tried to make an appointment with a therapist but because it was during a pandemic there were no available appointments. I felt a sense of betrayal that life had let me down. But life didn't owe me anything. The universe wasn't conspiring against me, but neither was it going out of its way to bring me good luck. I had to push the memories away of the uninhibited moments of being able to just go and do now that the kids were grown. I had to accept this for what it was; our life was changed.

There were parts of me that needed to be brought back. I had to start taking care of myself and that didn't mean physical only. I had to let go of handling everything and realize that I couldn't be everything to everybody. I needed to give myself a large dose of self-compassion and to know that *I am enough.* I had to be brave enough to stop sometimes and sit down in the middle of it all. Author Annie Lamott said about cultivating your rest and sleep. "Almost everything will work again if you unplug it for a few minutes, including you."

Too often, we believe that we are the only ones going through tough times and climbing an uphill battle. I just never paid attention because it wasn't happening to me. I tried to exercise but I was still nursing pain from injuries. Instead I read articles and books voraciously of those who faced adversities. Joan Lunden co-host of Good Morning America from 1980 to 1987 and author of eight books overcame cancer and was sandwiched between raising older and younger children and was a long distance caregiver for her mother. Actor Michael J. Fox stated in an article about the journey with Parkinson's disease that he became an old man at age 30. Christopher Reeves who played Superman in the movies

(1979- 1983) fell off a horse in a riding accident and became a quadriplegic.

I needed to find peace so I filled my back patio with potted flowers. I always enjoyed being outside and it kept my mind busy. It began to lift my spirits.

I returned to journaling something that I hadn't done in almost three years. I was the book coach and helped others through their writer's block and was now unable to write. Mostly, I was too exhausted and it was an effort. I wrote to understand my life and figure out who I was and who I would become. I began to fill notebook after notebook. I had lost myself in being a caregiver. *Did being a caregiver hold more importance than being a wife?* After all, the wife implied a 50/50 partnership, but what happens when the wife is in charge of it all 24/7. *Should I add caregiver in parentheses behind wife? Wife (caregiver)?* Or is a caregiver unimportant in the way of the world and just another responsibility added onto my overall growing list.

Eventually, the words turned into more coherent thoughts. I started to write a book, a memoir/self-help about being a caregiver because as Brené Brown author of five #1 New York Times bestsellers states "One day you will tell your story of how you overcame what you went through and it will become someone else's survival guide." I want to help others write their stories about overcoming their adversities because any of us can either let the circumstances control us, make us victims or we can overcome our adversity and become the hero of our story.

Writing has helped bring back hope that there might be better tomorrow's.

I read Joan Didion's book *The Year of Magical Thinking* in which her husband died and her daughter was in the hospital in Intensive Care also fighting sepsis. She said in an interview that writing the book helped her enter and leave the grieving period. "When you're totally consumed and you don't have to think about anything else. You have to work your way through the thing, again and again, until you reach the point where you can rid the memories of the power to make you upset."

The memories of those earlier days have been left in the past; our past, they no longer make me upset. I have worked my way through the shock and the grief of what happened to him; to us. Acceptance but not defeat has settled over me. For better or worse we're making new memories and rebuilding our life together.

Rebecca Camarena is an inspiring book writing and publishing coach. As a Book Coach, she has specialized expertise helping authors with all aspects of book writing; from vision to concept to writing and publishing.

She is known for helping experts, entrepreneurs, coaches, and others write and publish their transformational life stories.

She is an international Best-Selling author of the women's anthology book, *Out of My Comfort Zone: Stories of Courage, Perseverance and Victory*. She is also a co-author in *Embracing the Journey: Inspiring Stories of Hope, Healing and Triumphing over Adversity*.

Rebecca also has experience as a public relations coach for authors. She helped her clients achieve personal and business success, placing and winning book award contests, Amazon best-seller status, features in online National newspapers and more.

Rebecca is a wife (caregiver to her husband), mother and grandmother. She earned a Bachelor's degree in English Literature after raising her family. The beach is her happy place where she enjoys the sand, surf and sun. She lives in Los Angeles, California.

You can find Rebecca at her website; rebeccacamarenabookcoach.com.

Beyond the Diagnosis: Thriving as a Special Needs Parent

Lisa Ciao

They say that God does not give you what you can't handle. I have been heard to yell at Our Lord, really, you must think I am a bad ass.

After years of wanting a family, I wanted eight children; I was blessed with four children, three births. I actually had four miscarriages, so I did get my wish and will be reunited with the four babies not born to me in Heaven. I do long to meet them, and I know they will recognize me when I am returned home to Our Lord. I know this because I have read many stories of mystics who state that they have seen Angels and souls since birth and know that our loved ones surround us. I can feel the shiver of air that blows through my hair. Or the pennies left unexplained in places that had no pennies, or the feathers from Heaven falling on my nose in the Lube in London. I have felt all this and there was no way any of this could be explained other than the supernatural.

God has certainly lined my children in perfect order. G is my oldest then comes my twin boys and then my peanut, my baby girl, Queen O. They are all two years apart with dates of birth 27, 28, 29. I had been on bedrest and on Terbutaline as I had been in pre-term labor. Being on bedrest with a one year old is difficult to say the least. I was blessed with a wonderful support system, as my Mom came to stay during the week while my husband worked. My Mother-in-Law helped on the weekends.

I stopped the medicine the morning of June 29 and went into immediate labor. The twins were born that day, of course, they were 4 weeks early. I was rushed to the hospital and the operating room as a C-section was needed for a safe delivery. It was too early to deliver the twins naturally as there had been stress on the heart of twin A and we knew twin B was not getting enough oxygen in utero. Twin A's heart was doing all the work for his twin brother and it had been said by the Doctors' that he could go into cardiac arrest. Believe me I was scared and prayer was my lifeline. I'd lay in bed and asked God to bless my children, to give me a safe delivery and to prove the Doctors wrong.

I had twin to twin transfusion and still do not fully understand it all. I was given a choice to abort Twin B but absolutely could not even think of that. The Doctors painted a very grim picture stating all the horrible things that could go wrong. I'd always say you are not God, you don't know the outcome. The Lord prepared me for this because my previous work experience had been in a medical malpractice law firm. I learned not to take what the Doctors' said as law and have total, complete faith in Our Lord. Did I stumble in my faith, did I fail? I sure did, many times. I'd then remember the Cross Our Jesus carried to Calvary for us, the faith he had in his father and that HE held me in his palm. I was blessed with these babies for a reason and they chose me to be their mom. I'd tell myself to pull up my big girl pants and carry on. God has this.

As a kid I loved to dance tap, jazz, and ballet. I wanted to be a dance therapist upon graduation and work with special needs individuals. My mother told me that I was too sensitive and couldn't handle working with special needs. God has a great sense of humor and the last laugh because my whole world is special needs. My children's book, Anthony's Way, I AM ME! is about a little boy who always asks why he is special needs and his Mom's response as to all the reasons he is special, not special needs.

I was fortunate enough to listen to the direction that God placed in my heart to help my son, the people, doctors, and therapists all seemed to fall into place. My son's dad and I would ask a million questions and not take no for an answer, there had to be more ways to help. We had other children to compare my son to and I really didn't want to see the differences for the first six months. It was very hard for me to realize and see that he was different. I remember making an appointment to see my OB/GYN and asked him to explain twin to twin transfusion and all that that meant for my son's life. Again, I was not listening to my own self, that we don't know the outcome, only God does. Proverbs 16:9 says, "In their hearts humans plan their course, but the Lord establishes his steps." His response was to ask me if I was blaming him, but the reality was, I blamed myself.

In infancy my son had a bilateral hernia repair, hypospadias repair and bilateral tubes put in his ears, all with prolonged hospital stays due to lack of oxygen, his O2 saturation levels were very low and he came home needing to sleep in an oxygen tent. I'd crawl into his crib at night to sooth him and help him sleep.

At nine months we went to see a very reputable neurologist at a famous Children's Hospital. He had a terrible bed side manner and basically told me that I'd be lucky if my son could walk or talk. He called another Doctor who specialized in Williams Syndrome and I overheard him say, "I have a nine month old male spastic quadriplegic in my office, can you come down to see him?" Hearing those words, filled me with rage. Again, my steps were ordered by Our Lord giving me the knowledge and tenacity by working in that medical malpractice law firm for 12 years. I knew what those words meant. There was no way that was going to be true for my son!

I quickly picked up my son and told my husband we were leaving. I turned to that Doctor, with rage and indignation and declared that he did not know me or my Lord and assured him my son would walk, talk, run and play like my other children. And he did just that. I made that my mission, and unknowingly that became the mission of my other children, they led by example, pushing their brother to be the best he could be. In turn he did and does the same for all of us. The blessings are all mine, to have the constant innocence, purity, unconditional love, and trust in me is truly a gift. We have the same gifted to us by Our Lord. Am I accepting of it? Do I take it for granted or do I realize the meaning of all that is bestowed on me?

Through the years we were in and out of the hospital and calling 911 was a natural thing for my other children and the paramedics knew us by name. I remember all too well was being awakened one night by my son, who fell out of bed and was stuck between the wall and the bed, yelling to help him get out all the while his twin brother slept soundly in the other bed. The paramedics came, Arthur was his name, and he lifted my son up like he was a feather. My son, then escorted them to the front door, graciously thanking them and saying, "thank you for all you do to help me." My son recognized and was thankful when someone showed him kindness. These lessons are my daily life with my special needs son.

A few years passed and I'd get comfortable within him not being ill, growing out of the seizure activity and becoming a leader amongst his peers of individuals. He had an active social life as well as my other children and I was a busy mom. I loved it. To me there is not greater job, no greater joy and no greater gift than being a mother. My son is involved with Special Olympics, Hopes and Dreams Club which is a special needs acting group. Every year they put on a musical to the community's delight. There is Miracle League and Athletes Helping Athletes. We are truly blessed to have so many amazing opportunities to encourage being your best self and shining your light.

It all changed rather quickly! In November 2007, we started noticing changes in my son's behavior and it escalated the following in February. He regressed profusely, was delusional, manic and psychotic. It definitely was a scary time, again I felt frightened, alone and not knowing how to help my son. We were once again admitted to a famous Children's Hospital and this time it was for one month. We saw every team of doctors possible and there were no answers. Let's try this medicine they'd say, then that medicine. It was all a guessing game.

His system was shutting down, he had aspiration and developed Pseudobulbar Palsy. This is where you lose control of all the muscles in your face, including your jaw mouth, tongue, and throat.

As I rocked in my rocking chair, my son once again on oxygen, hooked up to all types of tubes, praying the Rosary, shouting to all the Angels and Saints, mad as all heck at God, crying, asking for help, my son said, "I see Mary!" I said "Mary who?" His response was "duh, Mary the mother." To this day, I laugh hearing his voice state this. It keeps me going that I am never alone knowing Jesus, Our Holy Father the Holy Spirit and the Blessed Mother are with us always. I did ask him what Mary was doing and he told me that she was crying with me, that she had her hand on my shoulder and was standing directly by my side. I asked what she looked like, and he said that she had a blue long dress with a hood on and she was pretty. You may say, "Oh, he was delusional, psychotic." I say he is pure and can see things we can't. I hold comfort in that and hold onto that, those words for dear life. I remember thinking if the Blessed Mother was here than her Son couldn't be too far behind.

Those days were a blur and one rolled into the next with everyday a new symptom, and it broke my other children's heart, especially his twin, to see him that way. It was days of fighting Doctors to listen to me. I knew my son and what is best for him. Sometimes, I think that my other children suffered a lack of attention from me. I feel guilty in that but then I realize that we all did the best we could. That is all we can do in this life, do our best, be our best and touch the life of another person.

I believe in our Heavenly Father and the fact that he is calling me to have Faith, to Trust and that it is all for the Glory of God. Today, my family is where we were after those years that shook us to our core. I know that we will get through and pray daily for the ability to hear Our Lord's voice, to see the direction he is leading me to and through and to be still and know he is God!

Lisa Ciao is the President of Maid For You, Inc., an independently owned professional cleaning company that has provided exceptional service and value to her community over the last 20+ years.

A Bucks Happening List and a Hulafrog's Most Loved award winner, one of HireHaven Top 25 Home Cleaners in Pennsylvania, a Best of Bucks award runner-up, and proud supporter of various local charities.

She believes that everyone should have a R.I.C.H. life; through her services, your home becomes a dwelling that is relaxing, inviting, and cozy so that you can feel happy.

Lisa is the founder of the nonprofit Anthony's Center for Independent Adult Opportunities and author of *Anthony's Way, I AM ME!* a children's book that advocates for children with intellectual disABILITIES. It takes the reader on a journey through her son's life who has Kleefstra Syndrome and shares about his special needs and uniqueness. She is also a co-author of the anthologies *Dust to Salvation: Stories of Grace, Love, and Redemption in the Midst of Jesus Revealing Unexpected Miracles* and *Embracing the Journey: Inspiring Stories of Hope, Healing and Triumphing over Adversity*.

In her free time, you can find her on the dance floor.

To learn more about Lisa, visit her at facebook.com/lisaciaoauthor.

A Lion's Roar: Transformation Through a Kundalini Awakening

Tania Elena Gonzalez-Ortega

There I am sitting in the "Peace Dome"- a funky hippie-like geodesic dome set in the nook of some pine trees at the edge of the grounds at the Sivananda Ashram in Val Morin, Canada, thousands of miles away from my home. My heart is broken. My long distance boyfriend dumped me. I thought he was the one. I am hoping this yoga teacher training will heal me from the deep ache that I've been carrying in my heart for the last six months.

As part of the training I am initiated into a mantra: "Om Namo Narayanaya." I have been instructed to mentally repeat the mantra silently while focusing on my third eye in order to meditate, and this is to be my personal practice for the rest of my life.

So, sitting on my meditation cushion in the peace dome by myself, I begin to meditate as I have been instructed, "Om Namo Narayanaya, Om Namo Narayanaya, Om Namo Narayanaya."

My desire to discover "enlightenment" has always been very strong. There is something more to this world as we see it. I had glimpsed moments of "no mind" before and the feeling was indescribable. This is what I have been searching for - permanent peace.

My spine is erect and I am 100 percent focused. I can feel my mind wander from time to time, but I keep bringing it back to the mantra.

About a half hour later, I feel a rising of energy. My body feels like it is floating. I can see a golden light start to flood my being. This feeling of going higher and higher is intoxicating and I don't want it to stop. "This is it! Enlightenment! Keep going!" I think to myself. I stay with the energy which continues to build, until all of a sudden I hear, out of seemingly nowhere a tremendous lion's growl. The sound completely engulfs me, penetrates every cell of my being. I have no more sense of me or my body.

Immediately I stopped the meditation wondering, what just happened? What the fuck was that? I am terrified thinking I had tampered with something that was not to be tampered with and that something has gone terribly, terribly wrong. I gather my things and quietly leave and choose not to speak a word of it to anyone. I decided to pretend it didn't happen. I let it go. Little did I know I had just experienced a spontaneous Kundalini Awakening.

I go back to my yoga teacher training and complete it. I received my certificate and I made the decision to commit myself to the organization. With the fear of God in me, I approached Swami Sita of the Sivananda Ashram in San Francisco and asked if I could serve as full time unpaid staff in their center, receiving only room and board. She looks me up and down, trying to size me up and accepts me as a full time staff. "Are your intentions pure?" she asks. "Yes," I humbly replied. I made my way out of Canada and back to San Francisco – home.

This feels like a new life to me. Leaving behind my heartache, choosing to live a life of "purity" and spiritual practice feels so right. The 4 weeks of yoga training has opened my body in ways I had never physically experienced before. I just want to clear my past and start a new chapter.

A week passes, and something shifts with my physical health. I am scared. My digestive system begins to shut down. I am not able to have a bowel movement for days (which turns into two years of having to rely on enemas and laxatives) and I am starting to lose weight.

I am doing everything I can to ignore what is happening to my body. I try to just think it will pass, but on a much deeper level I know something is seriously wrong.

I said to myself, "I have to keep going; there's no turning back now; I don't want to fail."

I keep to my strict schedule of meditating every morning with the ashram residents at five am for an hour, have breakfast, do yoga, teach yoga, execute marketing materials, maintain the supplies of the kitchen, cook and clean. I am finding that I am going to bed close to midnight every night after following swami's orders. My exhaustion and physical issues are surmounting.

I keep trying to ignore the fact that my health is spiraling out of control. A couple of months pass, and my menstrual cycle completely disappears. I am noticing when I go to brush my hair that it is literally falling out in clumps. My ribs are starting to show and I am noticing a dark brown dry spot of skin forming at the base of my spine.

I begin to have strange happenings during my sleep. During my sleep I feel like my body is being electrocuted – like my nerves are being completely fried. It is painful. These waves of electricity that come out of nowhere start to happen more frequently and I notice that after the shock, I find myself astrally projected into different realms, out of my body. These night time travels are terrifying and painful. I hear and see terrifying things – demonic laughter, chariots of horses, strange lucid scenes that make no sense.

The weeks pass and I begin to experience panic attacks. My breath feels short. There's not enough air. I reached out to swami for help. "I can't breathe, I think I'm dying." She scoffs at me. I can feel her thoughts, "She is pathetic." She just wants me to keep working. Free labor after all, more money for the ashram. She clearly does not care even though she can see I am losing weight by the week. I have gone down to 112 pounds (I was 135 at the beginning and am 5ft 8inches tall).

It is now a year in. The swamis can no longer ignore what is happening to me. My health and nerves are shot. My mind is ravaged with anxiety and chronic fatigue. They decided to make my load lighter by moving me to their ashram in Grass Valley, thinking being in nature would help. Just get me out of the city.

The "farm" is beautiful. Green with rolling hills and oak trees located in Grass Valley. But things only worsen. The night time electrocutions continue. The amount of inner turmoil only continues to surmount. While in my room at night I begin to experience spirits coming to me trying to take me out of my body. I begin to hear a continuous "OM" sound in my ears at all times of the day.

In yoga they talk a lot about austerity being part of the path of yoga, so I try to convince myself that I am on the right path and this is part of it. I just need to endure and surely things will become clear. I keep praying, meditating, and doing yoga every single day. I do my duties. I follow the rules.

But one day, a female guest of the ashram approached me and said, "You need to get out of here. You are dying." The look in her eyes spoke volumes. This is the first time I actually feel someone showing care and concern for me, and I know she is right.

Part of me kind of likes the sound of dying at this point, but I take her words seriously and ask the swami if I can go back to San Francisco to be closer to my mom and just be part time staff and try to get a part time job.

I returned and secured a part time job at a local non-profit. I continue to participate in the activities of the ashram, but nothing is shifting. My soul now has left me completely. I have zero capacity for joy, connection, contentment. I only feel fear, anxiety and depression. I feel completely dead inside.

My mother is now deeply concerned. It's been two years now watching from afar what is happening to me. She tries to talk to the swami who tells her I'm fine. "Nothing is wrong. Tania only needs more money," says Swami Sita.

Of course my mother does not believe this. After meeting with the swami, she comes to me in my room and asks me, "Tania, do you want me to take you home?" Tears well up in my eyes. I start to shake and sob. Of course I say yes. God, yes.

I leave the ashram that very minute like a prisoner on a break out. I leave most of my belongings. I leave a note for the swami and all the money I have left in my bank account around a thousand dollars. I don't want her anger which is often displayed to all of us staff members on a daily basis. I want zero ties.

Seeing my completely distressed body and mind, my mother checked me into a psychiatric hospital for three days. I willingly go. I am up for trying anything at this point because now I am completely suicidal. The doctors gave me a couple of pills. I see several other people who seem crazier than me. After the second night, I leave.

I know I have to do something different. My uncontrollable sobbing and continuous anxiety are only overwhelming my mother. I ask her to take me to Tucson to live with a long-time family friend. I got a job at a bakery. My mother signs me up with a psychiatrist who puts me on six different drugs.

Eventually I got my own little studio apartment. The psychiatrist tells my mother she is surprised that I haven't got hooked on drugs by now to try and escape my anguish.

Each day feels like ten years. I finally gained some weight thanks to the psychiatric meds and working at the bakery, but at this point, nothing is helping the anxiety or depression. I seek help from a counselor, an acupuncturist, doctors of all kinds including from Eastern and Western medicines. My brain feels like mud. My digestive system is still a mess.

One night at my computer I came across the writings of St. John of the Cross on the internet who wrote The Dark Night of the Soul. I read the original text carefully and can recognize that this is very relevant to me. And sadly, it basically summarizes once you enter the Dark Night of the Soul, your body/mind/spirit is being purified and that the only way out is to surrender to God. When and how the Dark Night ends is completely in God's hands. This becomes the only idea I can hold onto.

I can't help but to continue to pray, and eventually amazing synchronicities start to happen. My aunt and uncle happened to be traveling in Pagosa Springs and connected with Peter and Rebekah Laue because they loved their sandblasted signs which expressed the love of Christ. Peter and Rebekah have an "Upper Room" in their home where weary souls can come and restore their body, mind and spirit through Christ. Peter has his own story with mental health issues and shares his story with my aunt and uncle. They in turn share with him what I am going through.

I end up at their doorstep, but only after I throw away all of my pills and state to God, "God, Peter is the last person I am going to seek help from. If this doesn't work, I promise to completely surrender my life to you, even if it means I become a crazy homeless woman."

The next three days end up completely changing my life forever.

The first night there I have a powerful dream: Peter and Rebekah are in the dream telling me to drink from the Water of Life. I drink. That night I sweat through my bedclothes and sheets. That next day, 2 men show up – friends of Peter and Rebekah. Peter gets up on the coffee table in his bathrobe with his sword waving in the air, "I name you Lady Liberty! You are free!" He repeats this several times, dancing up and down and speaking in tongues. I begin to laugh – I notice this is the first time I have laughed in 2 years. The two men then begin to pray over me in tongues and instruct me to do the same. This doesn't' mentally compute to me as just sounds like made up babble, but here I am. So, I decided to just do it – babble. To my surprise though, pain just literally starts to pour out of my body. I can feel it coming out of my mouth like black tar. This lasts only about five minutes, maybe ten.

I am not sure what just happened, but something has definitely changed.

The next day, I fly home.

That night upon returning I had another powerful dream experience. In the dream, there is nothing but black night. My soul returns to my body. I hear a female's voice say "Tania, are you okay?" I say wearily back to her, "I am a little beat up, but I am okay."

The next morning, I wake up only to discover, ALL of my anxiety and depression are COMPLETELY GONE. Two years of hell wiped out in one single night. For this first time in two years, I feel the trees again, the sun, the air. I feel joyful, happy, and elated. I danced in my room that morning.

Everywhere I go I feel the divine presence with me. This is bliss. This is peace.

My spiritual gifts as a healer and empath unfold. My body heals and I spend the next twenty years working with children, studying energy healing, and pursuing my art. I begin to understand astral travel and accept it as a part of my uniqueness and path to wisdom. My faith in God becomes unshakeable and I gain a strength within me after having gone through this that carries me through all of life's ups and downs.

I haven't entered another dark night since.

The realization is this: I Never gave up. God never gave up on me. I don't need to do or be anything to earn or deserve God's unconditional and miraculous love. This life is a divine mystery. Nothing is as it seems. Miracles happen.

Tania Elena Gonzalez-Ortega is a visual artist, Waldorf early childhood educator, and energy healer who always has passion for fine art, music, meditation, yoga, and spirituality.

As a child, she had a highly sensitive and empathic nature. After graduating from UCLA with a fine art degree, she dove into yoga, self-inquiry, and meditation by joining the Sivananda Yoga Organization as a full-time yoga teacher and staff member. She experienced a spontaneous kundalini awakening in 1999 which catapulted her into experiencing astral realms, spirits, telepathy, lucid dreaming, and other spiritual gifts while at the same time being forced to go through a grueling healing crisis that ravaged her physical, mental/emotional, and spiritual body. Her path to healing led her to the amazing discovery of the invisible and powerful realm of energy healing.

She trained with Reiki Master Mega R. Mease and Crystalline Consciousness Technique™ (CCT) founder Gia Combs-Ramirez. Twenty years later after perfecting her skills, she now serves others via one-on-one healing sessions and also teaches people how to heal themselves and others with energy healing. She now lives in Twisp, WA in the eastern slopes of the Cascade mountains.

You can learn more about her, her sessions, and classes at newearthconsciousness.com.

Grief and Loss: Hiding My Inner Pain After a Loved One's Death

Deborah Kos

I know that death is inevitable! It happens. I was aware that my father-in-law had some health problems. He fought them for years with vigor and conquered them! He even made it through brain surgery twice!

Little did I know that 2020 would end up being the craziest and wackiest year ever. I had so much hope for a fabulous year. It felt like it was going to be a year of renewal and great things for the future.

My father-in-law was hospitalized for an infection at the end of January. His infection was taking a long time to heal. The family and I made daily visits to the hospital.

In mid-March, 2020 life as we knew it changed. A pandemic the likes we had never seen before with a very contagious virus called COVID-19 caused everything to shut down from stores, restaurants, nursing homes, schools and more. Hospitals stopped allowing visitors. We were instructed to stay at home, abide by social distancing, and wear face masks for protection.

Around the end of March, he was released from the hospital to a rehab facility place. He had to stay in a rehab facility for six weeks minimum. He was not happy and wanted to go home regardless of what the doctor said. The family had to convince him that this was the right thing to do for his health.

During lock-down, new rules were in place at the rehab center. It was for everyone's safety. There were no visitors allowed, under any circumstances.

We tried to call him on the phone every day but half the time he couldn't hear the phone ring. The nurse always had to call us for him. My husband was really upset and was feeling guilty because he couldn't see his dad.

In mid-May, he was days away from being released. We were relieved that he would soon be home with us. However, it was not to be. The nurse called to tell us that he tested positive for COVID-19! We couldn't believe it! How did he get the virus? No one really understood what it was yet and how easily it could be transferred to others.

The whole family was in shock, including me. Poor guy, all he wanted was to get out of rehab. Three days, just three days before he was going to be released to go home, he got infected. Unbelievable! Why? It just seemed so wrong.

The rehab place sent him to the hospital and he was put on a ventilator. He was doing really well the first week of the infection. The second week his health was failing. My husband couldn't even go to the hospital to see him, and he felt even guiltier.

Day 12 of COVID-19, we got the call that we never expected. My father-in-law had died. It was a real blow to the family. "I hate you COVID-19! Why did you take my father-in-law? Why did you have to keep us from seeing him when he needed his family the most? I hate you! I hate you!"

I was experiencing shock, denial, anger and grief.

I couldn't even imagine what my husband was going through. He didn't want to talk about it.

It was such a powerful pandemic that took over the world. The world which seems like such a big place suddenly becomes smaller when a pandemic like this hits. It seems that everyone knows someone that has been sick or died.

We had to have an outside grave site service for immediate family only. The rules limited the funeral to 10 people in attendance. We couldn't tell my husband's entire family because there are so many and they would want to crash the outside funeral mass.

I kept trying to wrap my head around the fact that we suffered a death in our immediate family. I didn't want to do anything but just sit in a chair and grieve. I was angry, disgusted, and couldn't process his death. No one knew my inner pain or that I needed to heal too! I hid it from everyone!

I kept trying to be strong for my husband for when he wanted to talk about his dad. His guilt of not seeing his dad was really weighing on him daily.

I cried and sobbed on and off for about two weeks. My husband never knew how hard I was taking his dad's death. I wasn't my normal happy self. I hid it from him because he was having a hard time with it too, especially since he was restricted from seeing his dad during all this madness.

After a week of just sitting in the chair and dwelling about COVID-19 and my father in law's death, I knew I had to stop. I finally talked myself into getting off the recliner and getting back to work. I buried myself in my business hoping that I could get out of the depression I was experiencing. I needed to start living my life again and be there for my family.

I was beginning to process his death. I wasn't happy about it but the anger and the frustration were slowly disappearing.

I just had to get back to my normal life. I wasn't alone. My family was there to support me.

I pulled myself together because my father-in-law would have wanted me to so that I can take care of his son and grandson. I wanted to be there for them to get through this rough patch in life.

One day, a friend sent me a message and we talked at length about my father-in-law's death and it hit me like a ton of bricks. I was glad that I was home alone because I burst into tears.

After I pulled myself together, I realized that crying was exactly what I needed.

Grief just sneaks up on you when you least expect it. It feels like a heavy weight in your chest. There was also a time when I was being interviewed and the interviewer mentioned my father-in-law's death and then it hit me. I was trying so hard not to cry and tried to forget what she said and go on with the interview.

My family and I had to deal with the fact that the virus was something we really didn't understand and that it can kill anyone. The anger and grief of death before the person's time was up is very real. I believe it takes longer to process an unnecessary death from a virus that had no warning signs.

I learned that COVID-19 is vicious! I also learned that things would never be normal again for a long while. Life circumstances changed in the blink of an eye whether I liked it or not. I had to learn to put one foot in front of the other and go on with living. However, life is just way too different now.

I will never forget the COVID-19 year and how it took my father-in-law. I know my family and I still need time to heal and I am ok with that! I am taking it one day and one holiday at a time.

My father-in-law's birthday was three weeks after he died. My husband and I, along with our son, went to visit his grave site. My mother-in-law who lives in a nursing home was still angry that she lost her husband and refused to go to the grave site. My in-laws were married 57 years and had three grandchildren, two from my husband's brother and our son. She wanted to be with her friends and we didn't want to force her to go to the cemetery because she wasn't ready.

It was really sad and I could tell that my husband was really upset. We stayed about 10 minutes and went back home. He called his brother, but his brother didn't want to talk on the phone or about his dad. He was having a hard time dealing with his dad's birthday too.

I made my husband's favorite chili, homemade garlic bread and ice cream for dessert that night for dinner to help ease some of the pain. I was hoping his favorite foods would help to ease a little of the pain.

My father-in-law would have wanted us to go on but when I told that to my husband he didn't want to hear it. He wanted to be left alone and was pretty silent for the rest of the evening. He couldn't wait to go to work to concentrate on something else.

I realize now that I had to take the time to process my anger and grief but know that I had to try to get back to your life and can't just hide under a rug. The deceased never wants their family members to continually suffer through the grief of their death.

My father-in-law would have wanted us to go on with our lives and take care of his grandchild. He wouldn't have wanted us to keep mourning.

He enlisted in the army and one of his jobs was peeling potatoes. He was proud that he served his country. He was the nicest man in the world. He was also the quietest but he was funny. Everyone that knew him loved him. He was highly devoted to his wife and family and, that is how he will always be remembered.

I accept the fact that my inner pain may still be there and always will. There will be triggers like holidays or certain memories that hit my husband and I when we least expect it. Those memories will always be there. We don't talk too much about the virus or his death however, I'm hopeful that it will get a little easier to talk about all the good times the family had on holiday and birthdays.

My father-in-law left us with many precious memories. He lived a good life and it's my honor to keep his memory alive.

Deborah Kos is the owner of Deb's Decorative Life. She is a professional lifestyle blogger/author who helps busy entrepreneur moms with kitchen prep, organization & decluttering to have a simpler/easier way of mastering their kitchen so that they can spend more quality time with their families or doing the things they love to do.

She loves helping women by sharing her experiences on her blog. She wants them to lead their own decorative life.

Her articles are featured at Today.com and medium.com, kdhcoaching.com, and fourcolumnsofabalancedlife.com. She was also featured on the Lady Boss Blogger website.

She was also nominated for the Flawesome Award, which tells how she overcame her flaws and turned them into awesome strengths. She also was nominated for the Sunshine Blogger Award, the Mystery Blogger, the Blogger Recognition Award, the Versatile Blogger and the Liebster Award and the Fix Her Crown Award.

She is also a co-author for the book *Out of My Comfort Zone: Stories of Courage*. She shares her story about how pain helped her to start a blog business.

Her second co-author book is *The Beauty In My Mess Vol 2: Stories of Love, Learning and Living*. She talks about how she learned to love herself and start living her life again after being lost as a Mom.

She is married and has a son in college, and a Siamese cat. She has been blessed to be a stay at home Mom for 17+ years.

Deborah survived when her husband was unemployed three times in two years and she still led a decorative life.

To learn more about Deb, please visit her website at debsdecorativelife.com.

The Beauty of Life: Surviving Tough Situations

Sonika Krüger

―――――――――――――

"Ma'am I cannot promise you, that your baby is alive."

These words were spoken to my mother when she was rushed to the operation room for an emergency C-section.

And these words were the undercurrent of my life. Every thought. Every decision. Every action. It was driven by the pure instinct of survival. I never realized I was living in survival mode, fight, flight or freeze. My default was to freeze in the form of debilitating anxiety.

Let me get back to my story…

When I was a few days old I got diarrhea, most probably from swallowing amniotic fluid. This caused me to get colitis and my mom got septicemia in her C-section wound. She too was surviving and hoping to come out alive.

My parents were not allowed to hold me during those first few days of my life. I was lying in an incubator with an IV drip plastered to my head.

Even though I don't remember any of this, I have heard the stories. And these stories molded me into the woman I became.

My mom tells me very proudly that I was fighting every day for my life. And I agree with her, she had every reason to be proud. Yet, that those first few weeks of my life has really set the tone for the rest of my life.

A life of survival. This fighting for survival is exhausting. And it takes away the beauty of life. I wouldn't change anything about my story. In my life I have learned that I am resilient, and I am able to survive tough situation.

I was about two weeks old when I was released from the hospital. And I grew up hitting every milestone in perfect time. I loved to learn. I wanted to go to school so that I could learn to read and write.

Yet I cried myself to sleep for the first two years of school. I was afraid of my teachers. I was afraid of lunch breaks, because that would mean that I had to go out and make friends. I was afraid of everything.

Not knowing better back then I cried because I was afraid to leave my mom. She was like my security blanket. If I wasn't with her, life felt confusing and scary. Neither of us had the awareness that I was in survival mode.

My parents did an amazing job raising me. And I will forever be grateful that they are my parents. I was headstrong. I showed leadership qualities. I was a good kid. I was an "A" student. I didn't get into trouble. I didn't rock the boat. Like a good older sister, I looked out for my sister and making sure all her needs were met. I ticked all the boxes of a good and perfect child.

One of the things I enjoyed between the ages of eleven and thirteen was to ride my bike around the neighborhood. My friend and I would ride around for hours. Sometimes we would visit an old lady in the retirement village near our homes. Sometimes we would race other children from the neighborhood. It was so much fun. Blonde hair. Sun-browned legs. Fit and lean body. I didn't feel fear or anxiety when I was on my bike.

One Saturday morning my friend and my nephew and I decided to race one another. The saying "look ma, no hands" was me that day and that saying had a whole new meaning for me. I wanted to win. I went full-out that day. In an unguarded moment I wanted to pass my friend and my bike's front wheel collided with her back wheel. And I went flying through the air, with my bike still firmly attached to my tush.

I came down hard with my head first on the road. I think I passed out because there are a few minutes in my life not accounted for. My nephew rode as fast as he could back to my home to call my mom. Yelling that there is green stuff coming out of my head. My mother came running to me… she ran faster than my nephew who was still on his bike.

I got back up. Picked my bike up and started to walk back home. I am not sure how I got back home that day. I only have a small scar left of that day. When I think back to that fateful day, I became aware of the resilience that is knitted into my DNA. That happened when I was about twelve years old.

Four years later, I was in an accident. Rather foolish of me I wasn't wearing my safety belt. It was a head-on collision in an older model car, without ABS brakes or airbags. My poor head again took the hardest knock. I had to wear a neck brace for a week. And my knees were knocked blue. Again, I came out of the accident unharmed.

I think the Lord was now starting to lose His patience with me and was beginning to scream that I am to thrive, not merely survive. However I chose to ignore Him and found myself in an abusive, fighting for survival relationship.

There were so many bad moments in that relationship that I wished I could walk away. I stayed despite the whispering (and at times shouting) of the Lord. What is the saying, what you resist, persists?

I resisted all the warning signs even the subtle and obnoxious ones.

Later that year, I received a Divine and beautiful prophecy. It was said to me "I see you standing before women and bringing them to a place of healing." At sixteen I didn't understand it. I tucked it deep inside my heart and this became a mantra/affirmation in my life.

I felt called to ministry and I thought that this prophecy will become true once I stand in ministry as a Reverend. In my first year at varsity, I once again came face-to-face with death. I did au-pair work, two boys aged nine and seven. One afternoon when we got home, there was an unknown vehicle in their driveway. I asked them if they knew anything about it and they said no. My inner voice was shouting something was wrong, but due to my freeze instinct, I didn't listen. We walked in and were faced with eight armed men. Dangerous. Fearless. I live in South-Africa, and we are well known for the violent crimes that happen daily.

My biggest fear for that day was that my friend and I will be raped, and the mom will walk in her home finding all of us murdered. My friend and I were locked in the bathroom. And we began to sing. I cannot remember what we sang. All I know is that in the moment an indescribable peace came over me. The words of Psalm 23 "when I walk through the valley of death I shall not fear" came true for me that day.

The two boys were tied and a blanket was thrown over their heads. We weren't raped. We weren't murdered. We walked through the valley of death that day and came out on the other side. That fateful day was the last day I had such a near death experiences. However, I stayed in survival mode. I finished my studies. All the while, keeping that beautiful prophecy tucked into my heart. I was one of the lucky ones that found work as a Reverend.

In my ten years in ministry, I experienced some of the greatest hurts and heartaches in my life. When women stand in ministry she becomes a punching bag for men, women, and colleagues. Things like "you are too pretty to preach" were said to me more times that I can count. My one colleague would lash out on me when I tried to speak up for myself. If it was in a different work environment sexual assault and harassment claims would have been made. However in ministry a claim like that would have had no charge.

I have been in ministry for ten years. It was one of the biggest losses I endured in 2019 when I got retrenched. I loved to study the Bible and teach it to my congregation. I love to experience the beauty of baptizing a child and seeing the wonder in that child's eyes. I love to serve Holy Communion to my people. And all of that was just taken away. I mourned my loss in 2019. And I had great difficulty moving past that. I missed serving God's people. And just as I was on the journey of creating a new ministry, COVID and lockdown happened.

In 2020 my whole life fell apart. I remember evenings when I went to sleep with the thought, may I not wake the next morning, because I cannot handle the anxiety and fear, I cannot handle the fights and emotional breakdowns in my home anymore, I cannot see how my children are suffering and getting depressed because they are cooped at home.

I just couldn't handle it anymore. And the breaking point in all of this was the morning I realized I didn't even know that there is trouble in my marriage. An ugly problem that has reared its head again. I felt defeated. I felt hopeless. And I felt ready to give it all up.

All of the clever people told me to journal. I did that, yet I didn't experience any insight. I meditated, but the thoughts in my head made me crazy. I medicated myself just to survive.

My parents invited us to go to the ocean with them. A small town in the Westcoast. And I said yes but only because I didn't want to disappoint them with saying no. That was the wisest "yes" I have ever said.

On those white, sandy beaches, with the cold Atlantic Ocean at my feet I became deeply aware of the presence of God. On the second day while I sat with my butt in the sand I began to pray. Not nice and beautiful words, but raw and unfiltered. In that moment, I realized that God's peace was missing from my life, and I began to beg for it. I felt His rich, tangible presence next to me. In that moment I knew with a deep and inner knowing that all is well in my world.

My journey to deep healing began in late December 2020. I am celebrating that day as a monumental shift in my life. No, my life and circumstances didn't miraculously change that day. I still didn't realize that I was stuck in survival mode. I was however learning to surrender. Being in control is a way of surviving. When I control the situation or the outcome there won't be any surprises that can scare the life out of me. Surrendering is a process for me. I honor myself each day to take it moment by moment.

My word/phrase for 2021 is Arise and be everything I am created to be. Like a phoenix I am arising from the ashes that burned me. It is easy to

become scared about the fire that is burning within and around me, because survival doesn't just stop the moment it is realized.
It is a daily choice. To thrive and to not merely survive.

When I look back at my life story there are a few fundamental truths or lessons that stand out to me. This is the exact moment where I am to be. All that has happened in my life was thoughts, decisions and actions that brought me to this place. I am to honor the moment. If I am not happy with this moment it is within me to make the next moment one that I am happier with.

I have already suffered in the past moments. I don't have to continue suffering. Yes, some of the experiences have been very traumatic and had a deep and profound impact in my life. Today I believe that that moment has showed up as a teacher. What can I learn from that experience?

Time is of the greatest essence in my life. I have learned to give myself time to heal. Just as a scab needs time to heal, so does emotional scarring need to heal. Healing takes time. It's taken me 35 years to get to where I am. I didn't rush and wasn't fearful about missing something.

I was for the longest time felt shameful for asking help. I feel that it was because of my need to control the outcome. I am a Coach and a Reverend. I should be able to help myself. Right? Nope, not right. When I was tangled in my mess, I couldn't find a way out of that mess. With help I received a different perspective, and I was given tools to untangle the mess of my life. Today I am lighter because I said yes and asked for help.

It was my last resort. I wish it could have been first resort. I prayed and prayed as if my life is depended on it. Because my life was hanging by a thread and I never knew how desperately I was seeking God. I didn't get a clear-cut answer that day on the beach. My problems weren't solved that day. That day when I prayed my raw and unfiltered prayer, I received peace. The peace that my soul was yearning for. I came home that day, into the arms of a Loving Father.

I look back at my story and I am proud. I survived hardships and it took me a long time to realize what was actually missing in my life. Because of my life's journey, I am resilient.

Now that I am on the healing path I am arising and becoming everything I was created to be.

Sonika Krüger is a teacher from heart and a minister of trade with a M.Div in Theology.

Her ten years in ministry has allowed her to become a professional speaker and is now comfortable on and off stage.

In 2018, she became a certified Leadership Coach with the Leadership Academy SA. This allowed her to coach in the international space with the TRAIN-initiative in Uganda.

She believes ministry, teaching and coaching goes hand-in-hand. And enjoys developing these holistically and implementing it in her online ministry. Through her ministry she helps moms connect within, to God and their loved ones. Her ministry focuses on developing self-care rituals, creating strong family bonds all while having an intimate relationship with God.

She has been an author in seven collaborations: *My een woord... elke week uit God se Woord* (My one word... every week with God's Word), *Vroue van die Woord* (Women of the Word), *Nou is die tyd... om genees te word van emosionele bagasie* (Now is the time... to be healed of emotional baggage), *Waar God lei sal Hy voorsien, leer by vroue uit die Bybel* (Where God leads, He will provide, learn from women in the Bible), *Is jy doof vir God? Hoe om God se stem te hoor in 'n besige wêreld en betekenisvolle tyd met Hom te spandeer* (Are you deaf for God? How to hear God's voice in a busy world and spend significant time with Him.), *FOUTE wat (selfs oulike) MA'S maak! 40 dinge wat jy oor ma-wees moet weet* (MISTAKES that (even good) MOMS make).

Sonika is a mom of two beautiful children. She lives in sunny South Africa and enjoys trips to the ocean, even though she lives in the bushveld.

You can find Sonika in the online space by visiting her website at sonikakruger.com.

Body Confidence: Loving the Girl in the Mirror

Emma Jayne Lions

I was an extremely thin child. So thin that during a storm, a strong gust of wind once blew me down the street! I was also a sick child and rarely ate much. I seemed to catch whatever was going around, no matter what it happened to be.

Mom asked doctors to find out why I didn't eat and how she could make me. After a number of doctors told her to 'just let me be', that I would 'eat when I was hungry', and that I would be 'okay' Mum eventually gave up. She tried so many things to get me to eat over the years but nothing worked long term. At one stage she even gave me vitamin C tablets before meals, telling me they were special lollies to make me hungry. This worked for a while - the placebo effect can be an amazing thing.

Food has always been a big issue for me, for obvious reasons, and so has my stomach. I have always had a 'tummy', which was considered cute as a child. Everyone would comment on my 'cute little potbelly'. I was a skinny little girl with potbelly and it was cute, until I hit my teens. Then suddenly I was told I had a 'fat gut' and I needed to lose it. I was no longer cute. Now I was just fat.

As a child I didn't have any issues about how I looked or what I ate. I couldn't understand what all the fuss was about? I was a small eater and it only took a small amount of food to fill me. My favourite food at the time was Kraft cheese singles and one slice was enough to fill me for at least four or five hours. I thought people were making a huge fuss over nothing. Until I turned 12, went to secondary school and the real problems started.

I was seven years old weighing around 48 kilos and I thought I was fine. I was eating the same kinds of food, did the same kinds of activities but suddenly, overnight it seemed, my family decided I was anorexic. I had no real idea what that meant at the time and thought it just meant that you threw up after every meal. I wasn't doing that so I couldn't have been anorexic.

My parents told me to start eating because if I didn't, I would end up in hospital, being fed by tubes. They threatened that I would be all alone because no one would come to visit me. And I would die, just like Karen Carpenter - didn't I take any notice of that movie?

After a few months I got sick of fighting everyone and was tired of being told I was sick when I wasn't. I decided to 'show' everyone I was in control, not them. I did eat and I was going to prove it. But I would be the one deciding what and when I ate. And it was then that the binging and secret eating started. Some mornings I would really struggle to eat all the food I put in front of me. I would save up my pocket money and would buy three or four dollars of lollies to eat on the way home from school, which was a 15-minute walk. What I didn't eat on the way home, I would hide in my bedroom to eat late at night. I would eat very little in front of other people, then stuff myself when I was alone. I remember being so desperate to binge at one point, that the only things in the house to eat were cheese slices and apples, it's probably the healthiest binge in history.

By the end of my first year of secondary school my weight had ballooned to 60 kilos and my family decided I had gotten too fat. I had gone from being 'anorexic' at 48 kilos to being 'obese' at 60 kilos according to them, and feelings of disgust for myself and my body started to kick in. I was told repeatedly that I was too fat, that I needed to lose weight, to go on a diet, to skip meals - it would all do me good. I started to believe what I was being told and started to see myself as too fat, too ugly and too stupid. I was so confused and for a long time hated my parents. In my mind it was all their fault - if they just left me alone I would've been okay. But they hadn't and I wasn't.

I was now 14 and the negative body image and eating disorder that was forming was starting to take its toll. I didn't know it at the time but I was setting up a cycle that I would continue into my 40's. A cycle with three stages: (1) do no exercise, eat what I like, don't care how I look: (2) feel like a huge, fat pig, go on a diet and start exercising like crazy; (3) come to my senses, stop the diet and exercise, stuff myself with food, get depressed, eat more food, and give up; and then repeat the cycle.

I was starting to identify with the anorexic mindset. I totally understood the thinking behind it. While other people sat around wondering why someone would want to starve themselves to death, it made complete sense to me. I couldn't explain it to people and they just didn't understand. But I got it, it was so simple. The desire to fit in and to prove others wrong. To prove you can be thin and beautiful and perfect. To prove you're right and to prove you can be like others. The right to say "See, I can lose weight; I do have will power; I can be as thin as you want me to be; I don't have any fat on me; I am that good; I am that thin." The only thing I didn't see was the connection to self-worth.

It was also during my mid-teens that I realised I had an eating disorder. I had read an article in a magazine that talked about binge eating disorder and how researchers and health professionals believed many people in weight loss groups suffered from it, and it hit me, that is what was wrong with me! I binged regularly with compensatory measures. I had thought I was bulimic because they manifest the same, only I wasn't eating the normal amounts during a binge to qualify as bulimic. I felt happy reading this article because there was a name for what I was doing and I had a real condition which meant it wasn't all in my mind. I was so relieved and quickly told mum and asked to go to the doctor. Mum agreed and we made an appointment but unfortunately for me, we never got there.

On the way to the bus stop, mum and I had a fight. She told me it was all in my head and there was nothing wrong with me except that I had no will power and was looking for an excuse to be lazy and not have to lose weight. As we walked back home, I decided never to mention my eating disorder or confide in my mother again.

Leaving home at 19 was a turning point for me in terms of my body image and eating disorder. I still hated my body but I was free. Free to eat and do whatever I wanted and that's exactly what I did - eat. Unfortunately, I ate junk. I realised I could eat what I wanted and when I wanted without being criticised or picked on or told how fat I was and I loved it. Sadly, so did my body and in 1996, I weighed 80 kilos. I couldn't believe I was so fat. My clothes didn't fit me and I had rolls of fat everywhere. I felt disgusted!

I started to diet again, which of course didn't last. At one stage my mum even tried to make it a competition to see who could lose the most weight in a set time. I told her I wasn't interested in competing against her and she told me I was just afraid I would lose.

Then one Sunday I decided to go for a walk. I felt good when I got home and decided to start walking each morning before work. I honestly never thought I would actually get up and go for a walk at 6am but I did. I wasn't on a diet at this stage, I simply made the decision to exercise and eat what I felt my body needed at the time. It was amazing. Within a couple of weeks I was eating a quarter of the junk I had been eating. I was cooking proper meals at night, my clothes were fitting better, and I started to feel really good about myself and my body. I'd never experienced this before and I never wanted it to end.

But like all good things, it did. I had to move back home with my parents when I lost my job and with the move came the old dieting and self-hatred cycle. This was when I should have seen the connection between my body image, eating disorder and worth, but it hadn't clicked yet.

After losing my job, I made the decision to go back to the university. At the time, I was interested in nutrition and exercise, enrolled in a Human Movement degree. Looking back, I'm not sure it was smart of me to enroll in a degree that focused on sport, fitness, and the body. Although I'm glad I did!

There I was at 22, weighing 75 kilos, having hated sports at school and I was enrolled in a sports science degree, full of skinny 18 year olds, who loved to exercise, eat well and keep fit. I preferred to sit on my butt and stuff my face with comfort food. I hated my first day. I felt so fat and ugly and stupid and incompetent, I never thought I would get through three years. Somehow I did but not without moments of bingeing, self-hatred, excessive exercise, dieting and depression.

One of the main benefits of studying sports science was the amount of information and knowledge I gathered regarding body image and eating disorders. I also learned a lot about myself and my own problems. In my first year, while researching an assignment, I came across a questionnaire. I can't remember the name of the questionnaire but I do remember the results.

I had always thought of myself as kind of having anorexia, which the questionnaire confirmed. I knew I thought, ate, and acted like someone with anorexia but I was overweight, so I couldn't be anorexic. I also binged a lot, sneaking food and eating alone. But then, my binges weren't on the same scale as most bulimics, although for me, it was consuming a large amount of food in a short period of time. Generally, I didn't try to 'get rid' of the food I'd eaten, so I wasn't bulimic, even though I did sometimes purge my body through exercise, and I wasn't really binge eating because I didn't do it often enough. In the end I decided I was a combination of all three. While this information was beneficial, it didn't really help me to figure out what to do.

Like my degree, being a gym instructor was probably a strange choice for me but in some ways it was positive. There was indirect pressure to look a certain way, an expectation that all instructors are thin, fit and healthy with a perfect body but in my experience, that pressure came more from the public and my family than the workplace and my fellow instructors. Being a gym instructor taught me a lot about learning to like and accept my body for what it is and being a BodyPump instructor allowed me to prove just what my body was capable of.

My first year out of university while working as a gym instructor, I had another breakthrough. I reached a point where I was sick of hating myself, especially because I didn't look the way society said I should. Why did I have to be thin? What was wrong with being me? I was only a size 14, why was that considered fat? Who was society to say how I should look? I was only 25 and tired. I wanted to exercise because I enjoyed it, not because I had to. I wanted to enjoy the foods I wanted to eat, rather than what was considered acceptable. This idea worked well for a while and I did feel better about myself and my body but again, it came to an end.

In 2003, I moved to a new town, Horsham to work in health promotion. I thought this would be a great opportunity to start afresh. I would be away from all the negative influences I felt were in my life at the time and I could begin a healthy, active new life. It started well. For the first six weeks everything was great. Then it happened. I had a bad day at work where I realised the job and the town weren't for me and I had no support.

I started journaling hoping to help me figure out a solution.

***

Day 1 - "It's been a while since I've taken the time to write and a lot has happened. I haven't started a new life. In fact, I've just kept living the old one. I have a huge, gigantic roll of fat sitting on my stomach and it's disgusting. I wish I could go and run it off or something but I've got the flu. Part of me doesn't care though. Part of me wants to run and skip and do anything that will get rid of the fat.

I'm in a wedding in 6 weeks. My dress doesn't even fit me now. I look like a gigantic blue whale, I'm so fat. I've been trying to walk for the last 4 weeks. Most mornings I've actually gotten up and gone for a walk. Sometimes I can't because of work. But I've been trying. Last week on the shopping list I bought skim milk, low fat cheese, multigrain bread, diet ice cream and Diet Coke. Yes, Diet Coke. Can you believe it? I've been drinking Diet Coke and skim milk all week. Can't wait to get back out and exercise. Think I might start tomorrow. Just a nice slow 2km walk. I'll take it easy this week coz I've been sick. But next week I won't. I need to start running. I want to get into shape for a fun run next year. Need to lose weight and get fit and strong. I'm too fat. You can't run when you're fat. It's too hard. Too much weight to carry. I need to burn fat. I've got lots of fat that needs to go. I've gotta be thin. I want to go back to uni next year and become a PE teacher and I need to be thin and fit for that. I need to start now, need to lose weight. Need to stop eating, stop bingeing. I'm bingeing too much here. At least 3-4 times a week and no exercise. Just eating and getting fatter. Gotta stop, gotta lose weight, gotta be normal...

I've done it again. Know what I've had to eat today? Twisties and Coke. I was thinking of going back to Weight Watchers. I've got all the stuff here. Maybe that's what I need but at the same time, I think it will have a negative effect on me. My eating disorder is bad. I'm not anorexic, I'm not bulimic, even my binge eating doesn't really fit the criteria.

80

***

Things improved slightly for me when I had my children. In both pregnancies, I lost a lot of weight because of the morning sickness and struggled to eat throughout the day. For the first time in my life, my weight was a blessing. Carrying the extra weight meant I could afford to lose 12kg and 20kg respectively and know that my babies were safe and healthy. I gained a lot of weight after my first child was born, getting back up to 78kgs. I was happy though because I was eating and enjoying my new life. Being heavier suddenly didn't bother me and I had no plans to lose the weight despite the pressure I faced from my parents. I started to see my body differently. It was no longer something to hate and be ashamed of. It was now a vessel that had created two children and I saw myself as more than just my physical body.

As my children grew, I began healing. I started to connect my beliefs around my body and my worth with the stories I had been told growing up. I always believed that my biological father had rejected me because I was a girl and this made me feel unloved and unwanted. This shaped my own views of my body and my worth. As I explored this connection, I began to understand my eating disorder and my triggers. I began to heal.

But the real healing came in 2018. This was when my family and I gave up our home and most of our possessions to travel and live location free. And it became a major healing moment. There is a freedom that comes from facing your fears and going against the status quo. For the first time there was no pressure to be anyone other than myself. I didn't have to be there for anyone other than my children. We could come and go as we pleased, without having to answer to anyone or justify what we were doing. In this freedom I found peace. And lost over 15kgs in the process and healed my emotional triggers.

Body image, eating disorders and emotional eating are at their core, linked to our worth. How I saw myself and my worth is the key here. Once I understood that, everything else fell into place. I spent my life believing I was unworthy of love and success. My weight became a way of protecting myself and my eating disorder was a way of trying to control my world.

While the stories given to me by my family were the catalyst for the development of my eating disorder, body image and negative self-worth, my decision to leave my old life behind and live location free as the catalyst for my healing. In leaving the status quo behind, I took back my power. I began living life and saying yes to life and new experiences. I accepted my choices because they were mine and not governed by others. I was giving myself and my children opportunities to see and explore life without expectation.

I discovered my biggest fear around my worth at this time. I was afraid the stories I carried would be true. I was afraid that I might really be unworthy and undeserving of love. But in facing my fears, in letting go of the way I had been living, in allowing myself to be free, I found my worth. I found self-love and I found me

I am not cured but I am healed. I know what my triggers are and have strategies in place to cope without having to turn to food or self-abuse. I feel more confident in my body and no longer rely on the number on the scale to determine how I feel about myself. I finally see my own beauty. And while I do sometimes wish that I had learned all this earlier, I am grateful for my journey. It has been a long road but I have learned to value myself. I know what I am capable of and live each day in my power rather than giving it away.

Emma Jayne Lions is an Australian-based author and mother of two, living in Ballarat, home of the Eureka Rebellion, where she was born and raised.

Emma holds a Bachelor of Applied Science (Human Movement) degree, along with a Diploma in Publishing. Her list of writing credits include a research proposal (exploring the relationship between body image and exercise in female Human Movement students), and a submission to the Victorian Government's 'Parliamentary Inquiry into issues relating to the development of body image among young people and associated effects on their health and well-being'.

When Emma began university she discovered a talent for writing. In 2011, she moved into professional writing, specializing as a health and fitness writer. In addition to the numerous books, programs and articles she has written for her clients and herself, Emma has a number of books published on Amazon, including two works of fiction - *The Bond*, and *Imperfect Beauty*.

You can connect with Emma via her Facebook Page at facebook.com/EmmaJayneAuthor.

Darkness into Light: Breaking Free from Toxicity and Narcissism

Sabita Saleem

As a child, I had no idea that I became accustomed to chaos and craziness. My days were filled with bullying, crazy conversations, and mental and emotional abuse not from just one person, but many. I was in a constant state of fear that all of sudden, somebody would come and make fun of me, insult me in front of everyone, and add one more name to the list of labels they'd already given me, that once again, I'll be told, "You're making a fuss," "You're the problem child," "You're slow," "You steal all the joy from the moment," and a lot more.

To add to my confusion during what should have been my happiest and most carefree days, those who played the key role in creating and perpetuating the toxic environment would play victim. Every single time, I was emotionally manipulated to over-empathize with those who were harming my thinking, emotions, imaginations, and my image.

I had no one to talk to, and every time I tried to share what I was going through, I was told "You're being way too sensitive, it's not like that." I was told to stay quiet because after all, they are elders. They're angry, shouting at me, comparing me with others, shaming me, making me feel guilty was "justified." I didn't even have "permission" to react in the name of peacemaking.

Little did I know that I was the black sheep of the family not because I felt like the "messed up, wrecked-ball of confusion", but because I was "special."

On the outside, I excelled in school. I was a straight A-student in college and at the university, and obeyed every word released from their mouth. In fact, I had learned to win the medal of "the most obedient child" because I mastered to not cringe about my needs but only theirs. Their schedule, their way, and their will were supposed to be followed in the name of "discipline and honor."

On the inside, my thoughts kept entangling me more and more. The negative, demeaning voices kept rehearsing in my mind day in and day out. To say I was angry at the mistreatment would be an understatement. I'd have imaginary conversations in my head where I was responding to them with fierce anger and rage over and over again. Unfortunately, the war of words remained in my head and didn't reach my lips ever because I was taught to bottle up my emotions and push my feelings aside.

Their view of reality had taught me to distrust myself, discount my feelings and consider that my voice doesn't matter because it was unacceptable. I had learnt to stay quiet *all the time.*

As a child, I was taught that I'll be safe with my "dear ones." They were family. Although they are quick to explode with anger, quick to judge with prejudice, quick to turn away from me, they were "nice and loving" people.

It was beyond confusing.

Stress, anxiety and worry were profoundly affecting my life and every second was emotionally, mentally, and physically traumatizing. My only escape mechanism was to sink my face in my pillow and cry as hard as I could, but then, I also had to make sure that nobody sees my swollen eyes in the morning.

My birthday used to be the hardest day of the year for me. I used to look forward to it NOT coming. I felt empty, like a piece of trash with a meaningless existence. I was not needed or loved by anyone.

One day the harsh, belittling words hit me so hard that one day I picked up a knife to commit suicide. I was praying that God would please let me die but He didn't. He didn't even give me the courage to try it again, although I secretly kept asking for it for years. Well, ask and you shall receive…didn't work in my case.

The saddest part was, I had no wisdom to prevent future attacks of stress, worry and anxiety. As a regular churchgoer, all I knew was to pray Psalms 23, 42, 91, and 120 in my heart, but this question never left me, why are these scriptures not working?

Still, a little flame was burning in my heart, and I could see light in the darkness.

Despite the terrible pain I experienced with every breath of my life, somewhere deep inside, I knew I could cry out to the One, the God Almighty, who is always there, always listening. He alone had the power to bring me out of this mess. Yet another question that used to haunt me was, *if my soul keeps crying for Him, why doesn't He listen?*

Psalm 23 was the passage I could hang on to when I felt scared to death and had no one to hold my hand, to hug me, or to wipe away my tears.

Even though I walk through the valley of the shadow of death, I will fear no evil, for you are with me; your rod and your staff, they comfort me. Psalm 23:4, but why were these scriptures not working? Where is your rod and your staff, Lord? Why are you not comforting me? I'm scared. Where are you?

To this day, I can't recall the warmth of my mother, the touch of her hands which makes me wonder, *did my mom and dad ever wipe away my tears? Why didn't my dad take any step to let these horrible circumstances end?*

Over the next couple of years, the pain increased. My body got accustomed to staying in pain, and my immune system crashed. I was still on medication since childhood for an autoimmune condition and my doctor visits increased. The vicious cycle continued: visit yet another doctor and add a pile of stronger painkillers to the existing heap of medications to take. I was asked to try every remedy under the sun to experience relief which never came.

My mind, my emotions, my spirit and my body were hijacked. The enemy had created strongholds.

Surprisingly, I had faith in the midst of doubt.

I still remember that day of April 2009. I had a dream in which I saw the following decade, possibly more, of my life unfolding right in front of my eyes. I saw the spiritual reality of the people I would cross paths with and eventually how I would come out of darkness into light. Back then I didn't know it was a prophetic dream because everything I saw in it has literally happened–every person, each conversation. I'm only waiting to see the very end unfold where I saw the rising sun shining in my face.

During the next two years, I kept crying to the Lord to let the pain end.

I don't want to be scared anymore. I don't want to cry anymore. Can you please come and wipe away these tears? You promised, Lord! You know me, Lord. I go to church regularly. I pray all the morning and night prayers, the rosary, and I also read one chapter of the bible daily.

But there was no answer.

All of a sudden, something touched me. I knew it was Him; the one and only living God. I could hardly believe it, but it was real. I could see a hand holding my heart, blazing with fire right in front of my eyes. And poof…it was gone.

It's ok, I told myself. *Take a deep breath, Sabita. What you saw wasn't a dream. It did happen.* He did touch my shattered, broken, and fragmented heart. It felt like a one-second touch but it was the touch of a lifetime, indeed!

I had become a magnet for all sorts of abuse—mental, emotional, physical and even spiritual. Unknowingly, I kept giving more inches to the toxic people in my life and they kept taking miles. I was in search of peace but I found it nowhere.

Still, I hadn't realized that the narcissists in my life offered me the poisonous cup of a broken identity. I was fed pain, guilt and shame morning, evening and night to have an identity that was finely fragmented, deeply broken, and highly insecure.

I wasn't allowed to acknowledge the negativity that was happening in my life. Even though I was a daughter supporting the family financially, helping in the household chores, doing whatever I could at the workplace, I certainly didn't measure up to the sky-high standards of performance placed on me. I was considered a good girl only when I bottled up my emotions, remained voiceless and wore a smiling face despite everyone making fun of how I looked, thought, felt and acted.

I became more and more conscious of myself around people, especially the dear ones. With time, I stopped smiling altogether, it's better to say I forgot what smiling was.

My parents were working professionals and they were busy; they hardly had time for me. I had no one to share my pain with, except God. I wanted Him to be my Father, but I only knew Him as a heavenly father who gets angry, roars in anger and keeps track of my sins.

Over the next couple of years, it became clear to me that these people want me to depend on them financially. I couldn't even choose to earn money the way I wanted. I couldn't decide anything on my own because I was supposed to live on the terms of the elders. They made me feel it was a sin to keep working where I could grow while leaving the family behind. I was labelled, yet again. This time as a foolish, highly ambitious, and a superior one who doesn't care about her family. I left my job and went back home.

But, since my encounter with God, my hunger to know Him grew more and more. As I was unable to find Him in the Scriptures, questions started arising in my mind about miracles. I had seen testimonies of people who were healed and delivered, and the key aspect was that none of them was from the church or denomination I was from. I wasn't able to get this question out of my mind, *why are others able to get blessings from God but I can't. Am I not following the same God?*

While listening to the testimonies, I heard about a teenager who shut himself in his room and spent time in praise and worship to seek the face of God. I felt I had finally found a way to get access to Him. I did the same. At a fixed time, I would go to the room, sing out loud for 30 minutes to an hour waiting for something to happen. A whole new label was thrown in my face this time, "She's started a new religion. What is she doing in there? (Although they could hear that I was worshipping.)" The more I worshipped, the more the TV volume went up, and the more my worship time was interrupted with knocks on the door for silly matters. But I didn't stop.

I kept confessing my sins, every little mistake to God. I knew He knew it all, but there was a little voice reminding me of the wrongs I did. This went on for months, and I didn't stop there. I had a strange joy arising in me and I'd start worshipping God anywhere in the house in a loud voice. I couldn't control myself.

One night, I decided to sit down at 3 a.m. to pray. I was scared to death because I had heard that this is the peak time of witchcraft. I thought there would be demonic attacks since the warlocks and witches were active at this time, but I also knew God's blessings were inevitable. I was terrified, but I got up with the courage and sat down to pray. I turned on worship on my mobile phone and started worshipping along with it. And, man, I started seeing visions with my eyes closed—the good, the bad, the ugly, but I kept praying.

God was watching how my heart focused on Him and He sent help, a divine connection who answered all my lingering questions about God and how to receive the baptism of the Holy Spirit. With my sister-in-law's prayers, exactly on my birthday in 2016, the day I hated the most, I was baptized in the Holy Spirit, and it became the most beautiful and cherished day of my life.

The first blessing I received was a miraculous end to the excruciating headaches I used to have every day for all the days of my life. However, the three-strand cord of stress, worry, and anxiety wasn't broken.

From that time forward, my journey of knowing who I am in Christ began. Little by little, the strongholds started breaking through the power of the Holy Spirit. Divine connections kept coming, as part of my online work. They were there to guide me through the trials and temptations. The dreams and visions kept increasing, but I was also hindered in hearing God's voice due to sleepless nights and the excruciating pain in my body. Although I could hear God's voice, many times I would get confused and wasn't able to discern the spirit.

The word of God says that when you are born again, you are a new creation [2 Corinthians 5:17]. I knew that since I had accepted Jesus as my personal savior, and was baptized in the Holy Spirit, everything in my life should get well now, including my mind, emotions, and my body. While I accepted this biblical truth, I didn't realize that inner healing is a process that takes time and that part of the package is an increased set of trials and temptations.

Once again, my mind and my emotions were hit with a massive blow of spiritual toxicity. The so-called spiritual leaders who put a spin on the word of God, preach man-made theology, and misinterpret Scripture to suit their hidden agenda had control of my mind and emotions. *My people are destroyed for lack of knowledge [Hosea 4:6 ESV]*. The sad truth was, I had recently started my journey of knowing who Jesus was and, little did I know, I had entered the camp of the enemy, the wolves in sheep's clothing. The battle in my mind sky-rocketed to a point where I could see myself having all the symptoms of a nervous breakdown, even while I was on extended fasting. Add to the equation, the stress, anxiety and worry coming from the workplace where I was bullied for being a believer in Christ.

Thanks to God, He had His way of pulling me out of this agony. God took me to the UK and through a fortunate turn of events, finally, in mid-2019, God broke the back of the deception I was bound to. I parted ways with the "wolves" and started reflecting back on what I went through.

It was heartbreaking to see that I lived a life that wasn't mine. I couldn't believe the long-lasting, repetitive destruction of my mind, emotions and above all my identity by multiple people in the name of seeking money, empathy, compassion and using God's name in vain.

Two thousand twenty marked the year of receiving God's perfect love and getting freedom from the long-lasting fear. God heard my prayers and brought a true spiritual leader in my life. The brothers and sisters God brought into my life through this spiritual leader, after an intense season of spiritual warfare, gave me an understanding of the mystery of His love. I started my journey of finally resting in God. I heard a voice telling me over and over again, *the season of rest has begun.*

Although I used to have visions with Father God holding me in His arms, in July 2020, for the first time in my life, God revealed Himself to me as my loving father with a promise that He will never forsake me.

I kept receiving the same word from multiple men and women of God:

> That He's holding me in His arms like a baby. He's happy to keep me in His embrace. He watches over me every night. They told me that you're very close to God's heart.

While everyone loathed my presence all my life, finally, there's someone who is happy with my presence. Someone who is not looking for me to perform for Him, but He loves me no matter how I look or what I feel and think. No matter how many mistakes I have made in my life, here is the One who has accepted me the way I am. Finally, I have found someone who will not criticize, ridicule and insult me.

Is it even possible? I couldn't grasp the truth that someone could love me like this.

Since then, with every passing day, I could feel His hand on my head, His gentle embrace, and the endless demonstration of His everlasting love. It's His love that led me to accept that I'm His child. You are fearfully and wonderfully made [Psalm 139:14] is now a living Word for me.

The tears haven't stopped, but now they are the tears shed due to experiencing His love and anointing. As His child I have known what true love looks like, and He's touching me every day to release the hidden fear and pain so I can get completely filled with His love and presence. He has broken the mental strongholds. I am no longer in the bondage of sleepless nights and excruciating pain. The negative voices have been silenced. I'm moving forward in my calling as a Kingdom-focused entrepreneur. I'm standing up, boldly and courageously, through the power of the Holy Spirit for families and generations, and it's only the beginning.

His will matters the most because He's called me and I have said, *I'm here Lord, send me.*

My life has taken a radical shift. The strongholds have broken, restoration has started happening, and it will only get better from there. I am a testimony, standing here today with a restored identity able to renew my mind daily and let God heal me emotionally, physically and spiritually.

Sabita Saleem is passionate about simplifying complex concepts into practical action items to help build understanding and momentum. By creating an unusual match of simple yet highly practical approaches, she leads online entrepreneurs in building their personal and professional lives.

She's on a mission to help Kingdom-minded entrepreneurs unleash the power of life-giving words and Kingdom truth so they can rise above their limitations, situations, and circumstances by selling their ideas, stories, products, and services and impact lives and generations like they never did before.

In her spare time, she loves exploring and implementing natural solutions for self-care, healthy eating, personal organization, and living a better life.

To learn more about Sabita, please visit her Facebook Page at facebook.com/sabitasaleemauthor.

Inner Transformation: Death Created Space for Growth

Janine Shapiro

My father adored 'his girls' my sister, myself and my mom. In a lot of ways, it was this adoration that contributed to his death. Technically, it was from a spider bite but in reality, his heart was broken.

My dad was a larger than life, loyal, caring and committed person. He had a temper but he was always there to support us at school, in business, in life. He was an outgoing, very strong personality and was always willing to assist people.

Family was so important to my dad. He grew up in a large family. Then his mom died when he was very young, leaving him and his twin brother to be brought up in a boarding school with little family interaction. His father was elderly and there was no-one to take care of the children His parents were immigrants from Italy (his dad) and England (his mom).

He would bend over backwards to support family, friends, and acquaintances. He was very proactive in the community giving back where he was able. Having been destitute when he was young, he saw the importance of supporting others. He set this example of giving in all areas of his life.

He and I fought a lot as we were very similar in personality. In spite of this I always knew he loved me completely. He always had my back. His life, how he embodied the spirit of giving and charity, and all the other underlying pieces of memories have contributed greatly to who I am today. I have learned so much about myself, life and awareness since his passing. It was his death that created the catalyst of choosing to create more for myself within my own life and what some may say, to finally 'grow up'.

I had no car of my own for a long time. Where I was living there was little public transport which hindered my free movement to visit my folks as often as I wished to. I had my coaching business and healing, and I was not charging for my services in line with the value I was offering. I was still living with the belief that I must give more than I had and a few other beliefs which kept my mind in lack which contributed to a variety of difficult situations. These and other reasons are the catapult that has launched me into being a Mindset Alchemist.

My husband worked away from home during the week and came home on weekends and my daughter did what she could to help me in supporting my parents in small and loving ways.

Subsequently, my husband began working near us and moved back home full time. This was an interesting adjustment as well.

The children laughingly told him, "Dad, you are coming home into OUR routine, you are the one who will fit in and not the other way around." A very valid point as we accommodated him on the weekends due to not seeing him so much. This would not work on a day-to-day basis.

My dad had a severe accident, and he lost his car and his work due to his disability and he could not fulfill his commitments. This was a huge blow to him as he was now dependent on a very small pension and my husband, and I were not in a position to assist my parents financially.

Then my mom's car was stolen, and they had no transport. There was no public transport where they lived. They were also supporting my sister, her partner, and my nephew, financially. Neither had work and they moved in with my parents as a stopgap, supposedly.

At this point, I suspected my mom was beginning dementia (my mom was actually 'hiding' from events I only discovered afterward) and she flatly refused to go to the doctor about her 'memory challenge.' My dad supported her in this decision. With hindsight, he was just too tired to do anything about forcing her and in too much pain from a botched hip-replacement from the accident.

My dad had always been active and an avid reader. His eyesight was deteriorating from diabetes, which was being exacerbated by his pain. This was a tremendous blow to him. Also, with no transport, it was very difficult to get them to the library and back. I organized audiobooks for him for a while.

It was a time of mutual frustration and misunderstanding. This was due in part to my pride and, as I subsequently discovered that my parents were hiding from me what was happening with my sister and nephew. I do not blame them as I was still in the very early phases of my growth and transformation process. My dad transitioning was the catalyst that speeded up the process considerably.

When the spider bit my dad and he was hospitalized due to it requiring surgery and other treatment. He was eventually intubated, made a dramatic recovery, long enough to ask me to take care of my mom. As I reassured him, I would do my best to do so, I glanced at the cardiac monitor. I knew he would not be alive for much longer. His spirit left his beleaguered body a few hours later.

Well, this was a defining point in my life.

Did I ever mourn my dad? With hindsight I miss his perspectives, love, and support in the physical. I did not feel I had to mourn his passing as he had blessed me with so much and I knew within that it was his time to go. I was angry at the mess left in my lap. It was also a huge part of my journey and my growth.

My husband and I discovered some very interesting points that we differed on and some hectic flaws in our relationship that were about to be exposed. My dad's death and my husband's way of coping with this led to some serious growth in our life and our relationship. It is said that nothing changes until we or something changes. So much comes down to choice awareness and the actions we take.

I disliked how funerals made me feel and now I had the task of organizing one. I found out later I am an empath and pick up on people's energies. I discovered how to work with this, and it has changed so much for my life. I found my father's funeral an intriguing look at people, as so many of the people he had helped in his life, chose not to attend. It was also very sad to see how many friends of his had passed on as well. It was a very interesting point of view around the cycle of life. It was also a very good preparation for my mother's funeral two years later when only close family attended.

It helped me to look at what I truly place value on, the beliefs around these values and whose beliefs I was living and how true they are for me. I got rid of things that weren't benefitting me and became more aligned when certain perspectives were put in place.

With my dad's passing it created growth for me, revelation and tore my blinders off in a way that was extremely painful and yet completely humbling. It has led me to be able to be far more effective in my practice and my relationships.

It was extremely humbling to learn that my son and husband had been correct about my sister and partner as far as their lifestyle was concerned. They had also dragged my nephew into their addictive lifestyle. This had bankrupted my dad and the threats to my mom had kept him in line and supplying cash. They had all kept it secret from me as well putting up a good front. Well, I had ignored the warning signs and the insights of my husband and son. Who said ignorance is bliss? It is often just plain hiding away.

There were also other circumstances at play where my family and I had stopped celebrating various Christian based festivals. I regret my stance on choosing to not spend time with my folks on these days. I have dealt with a tremendous amount of guilt and shame, and it has really helped me understand the value of family time and building relationships, no matter the occasion and reason for celebration. It created far more compassion for others and a deeper understanding of community. My absence also created space for them to hide what was actually going on.

This had so many consequences for my mother's health and care and empowered me to grow through learning to listen to my intuition. Things came to a head when an anonymous phone call to the ambulance and myself revealed my sister was forgetting to take care of my mom, even though we were supplying food etc. My mom had had a stroke shortly after my dad's funeral. This was definitely a period of growth and choosing to change. I was extremely disappointed with myself and furious with my sister for the neglect. I also couldn't see how I would take care of my mom by myself.

I am so, so very grateful for listening to my inner guidance at this time as it really made a difference when dealing with the nursing home, the medical aid society and my sister's covert actions around my mother's financial affairs.

I had a profound realization after my dad died. If anything happened to my husband, my practice was nowhere close to being able to support my children and me. We would definitely have to reduce our lifestyle dramatically. I was not open to this, at all. This galvanized me into taking action and expanding my business to reach more people by taking it online. I saw the online space as the way of the future and one I could use more expansively.

It has been a journey of discovery in so many ways and aspects. I realized that I was living my husband's dream and not my own. This was a HUGE factor in my discontent and anger as I had known at a deep unconscious level for a very long time I was out of alignment with my gifts and mission.

I am a recovering people-pleaser and as such had worked on keeping him and the people around me happy. It was a painful realization to understand that no-one was happy, and my children had suffered emotionally because of this. Well, we cannot go back, and I made the choice to go forward. So far it is an interesting and often exciting journey.

I came to understand I am an empath, a medical intuitive, a psychic and a healer. I also discovered that I really had been hearing whispered guidance and that it was not just luck that I had been able to understand what was happening with people and occasionally appear to 'hear' their thoughts, it is a gift.

When I was younger, people would tell me I had 'magic hands. I shrugged this off, although I would massage the aching legs of the cycling club members as they asked. I would receive many compliments as they felt ease seep into their abused muscles. I would often feel as if there was more to know, to see, to hear and would feel frustrated that it eluded me.

My dad dying and my mom being debilitated by the stroke released me from what was holding me back from truly seeing and understanding my abilities and capabilities.

So, my journey began online and within myself. I began my online journey with wellness and weight management, moved to uncover my psychic and healing abilities and opened me to business and leadership skills I had been acquiring through the years from my reading, self-development programs and much more.

At first, my husband was bewildered at my handing him his dream and stepping forward into my own. The interesting aspect is that he had never owned his own dream. We are on a similar journey of discovery, and this has made for some lively discussions and greater revelations as to the reasons we had so many hassles in our marriage. It opened us to mutual respect, understanding and growth which is filtering down to our beautiful children.

My dad dying has led me to the freedom that I was unaware that I was seeking. It set me free from the bonds of being daddy's little girl and being able to step forward into the beauty of maturing into who I can be. It has allowed me to see where my mom was a healer and an empath, along with being sensitive. It has given me a determination to work with my gifts to help others rather than having to hide who I am, as my mom did.

My parents leaving has opened me to see infinite possibilities and the potential of releasing the magic within me rather than taking it with me to my grave. I am also working with the magic of helping others do the same which uses the gift my in me when I was very young, that of teaching. So many serendipities along the way have opened me to even more abilities and ways of adding to my life and that of others.

I had not realized the journey would take me into myself to discover who I really am and how I actually work. It has been a journey of realizing that there is so much for us all in life and that creating tops constriction any day. It is taking me on a journey of discovering further ways of healing to help my clients at a deeper level and aligned level.

I have met and still meeting women, and men, that are on journeys of discovery and growth that I am so delighted to help and others I learn from. It is a give and take, share, and celebrate the journey of support, discovery and consciousness.

My dad was loving and giving. I wished to be like my dad. I had to learn that I am worthy of charging for my services and that it adds to the other person to invest in themselves.

My mom wasn't aware of her empathic abilities and hid from people to 'protect' herself.

I was empowered to learn to be visible energetically as well as in the physical so that clients are able to see me and work with me.

I am so grateful to be learning alongside my partner, best friend and husband as we explore the dynamics of the relationship, business and energy together in our own way. We make room for each other's style of learning and support this for our greater growth and leadership capabilities. It is so awesome to be able to support each other's dreams and visions as we create and work on a common one simultaneously.

I am also able to, in part, understand my sister's choices and journey. I am so grateful to learn that each of us has a different soul journey and body experience. This releases judgement and allows for compassion while creating room for accountability in another as through their journey. This understanding has really helped me as a healer and a coach. My dad's passing was traumatic, yet it also released me to be able to face myself and grow into the woman I am destined to be.

Life is a journey, and it is in choosing daily how we are to show up that has given me strength to explore my path and purpose at a deeper level. This has become part of my mission - helping others to do the same in their lives. I love the person I am growing into and wish the same for others and am actively working on making it so.

Janine Shapiro is a Mindset Alchemist and Healer, and she helps ambitious, heart-centered, entrepreneurial women release frustration and feelings of being unfulfilled to move to their next level of success so that they can live a life they love with an income they enjoy.

Using her psychic and healing abilities and experience you are guided to take aligned steps to find where you are and reach where you have always wanted to be.

She started out as a qualified registered nurse, midwife, and psychiatric nurse.

Her love of learning and teaching now benefits her clients.

Her personal experience with health and back challenges led her to expand her healing practice into using integrative, holistic healing modalities.

It was through this journey that Janine discovered her psychic abilities and passion for helping women to understand the impact you have on your business and life with your thoughts, words, and feelings and transitioned into helping you achieve your next level of success through releasing your underlying fears and limiting beliefs and healing what is keeping you stuck to move to unstoppable.

Janine is a happily married mom of 2 young adults and enjoys exercise, reading, and creating. Speaking, sharing information, and helping people move to their next level of success in life are also passions.

To learn more about Janine, please visit her website at janinekathleen.com.

Empty Arms: Finding Joy After Loss

Laura S. Shortridge

Several years ago, when my mother was clearing out her house of 50+ years, she gave me a box of mementos. Among the treasures was an essay I had written in seventh grade English class. The assignment had been to write down what we wanted our adult lives to look like.

In addition to becoming a published author and teacher and other things that have also manifested. I found it interesting that I had written down, "I want to get married young and have six children." Very clear and specific. I thought it, I spoke it, I wrote it down. I didn't know anything about our inner power at that time, but I knew what I wanted.

I graduated from High School while still 17 and left for college a month later for the summer semester. It seemed I was always in a hurry to grow up. I'm not one to sit around eating bonbons; I love to take action.

During Thanksgiving break in my sophomore year, I had turkey dinner with a local friend's family since my home was over a thousand miles away. A few other college students from distant states had been invited, too. Among them was what I considered an "older man," I was 19 and he was a whopping 23. We clicked immediately.

We both had dates booked with other people for the next two weeks but as soon as we had our first free evening, we went to dinner and a movie together. Hours flew by as we stayed up almost all night talking. We became inseparable. So connected, in fact, that we were engaged 11 days after our first date and married four months later. Boom! At the time of this writing, we have been married over 40 years!

After our honeymoon summer, we decided to start our family. Our first son was born three days after our first anniversary. Our second son was born 20 months later. Then I suffered the first of many miscarriages. It seemed my body had trouble hanging on to them beyond the first trimester. I was infinitely grateful when our third pregnancy resulted in a healthy son born three years later.

The next pregnancy also seemed like it would be successful since I went well into the second trimester, but then I started cramping and bleeding. My older sister, who lived next door, watched our boys while my hubby rushed me to the local hospital. Shortly after arriving, I lost our son. We never got to see him.

I was in critical condition, and it wasn't until a few days later that I found out our tiny child had been incinerated as medical waste. I was devastated. While I took good care of our sweet little boys and didn't let them see my tears, when they were napping, I would melt into a sobbing heap.

I didn't know what to do with my grief. Not wanting to keep the sadness in our little family, I tried to push it down deep inside me. It was like trying to hold a beach ball under water.

My normally cheerful disposition clouded; I forced myself to smile. There were moments I felt like I was losing my mind. Perhaps I was. Both my mom and husband recognized that I needed to let myself heal, both emotionally and physically. The pain was too deep to simply brush it aside.

The remedy? Mom watched the boys for a week while hubby and I flew back to our old college stomping grounds. We literally took a sweet trip down memory lane.

We sat in the same booth where we had our first dinner date and hiked the nature trail we frequented during our short engagement. We walked around the campus, ate burritos at the Student Food Court, and watched beautiful sunsets.

We also talked. I hadn't realized how deeply the miscarriages had touched my husband. He had been so busy with supporting our family and snipping away at his PhD that he, too, had pushed his sadness and concern deep inside. Plus, he didn't want to add to my emotional burden. That week together was a precious time of healing and reconnection.

I was refreshed and renewed when we got back home. Filled with gratitude at being with our little boys again, I joyfully stepped back into motherhood. With the support of my mom and husband, I also made a commitment to finish my bachelor's degree.

It had always bothered me that I didn't have that certificate, even if I had consciously chosen to be a full-time wife and mother rather than pursue a career. I am not a quitter. Incomplete tasks bug the heck out of me.

There were two universities near us so after visiting both, I gleefully discovered that if I changed my major, I could get my bachelor's degree in only three semesters. I jumped in with both feet.

My parents only lived a mile away from the campus so I would drop off the boys on the way to class then visit with my folks when I picked them up on the way home. They loved being with Grandmother and Grandpa. It was wonderful to see the bonds between generations flourish.

A week after my last semester, I gave birth to our fourth child, a healthy baby girl. She was a few weeks early but with no lasting complications. After two more early miscarriages, my husband finished his PhD and we moved out of state for his post doctorate. There, our fifth child; a second healthy daughter joined our family.

Finally, my husband's schooling was complete, and we moved to yet another state where he became a Biochemistry Professor at a major university. I'm not sure why it took me so long to recognize the pattern but after another first trimester miscarriage, I realized that every time I had lost a baby, I hadn't experienced any morning sickness. Even with our tiny son.

So, the next time I had severe morning sickness to the point I could hardly function I was actually grateful! I was finally going to have the sixth child to complete our family. By then, it was more routine to have sonograms, especially with my history of miscarriages. To my surprise, my 16-week ultrasound revealed that I was pregnant with twins! I would only have six kids for a short time before jumping to seven. Wow! I was thrilled and a bit scared at the same time.

At around the halfway mark of the pregnancy, the morning sickness disappeared as usual, and I was able to rejoin our church choir in preparation for a Christmas program. The finale was Handel's Messiah, which is one of my favorites. I remember having the alto part mostly memorized and was singing it as I went out the front door for our final rehearsal a few days before Christmas. I was so focused on the song that I didn't notice there had been a light drizzle that remained frozen on the front steps.

As I headed for the car, BAM! I slipped on the ice, landing hard on my bum. My husband heard me cry out in pain and helped me back into the house. I lay writhing on the couch while he called my doctor.

Before he got back to me, I had to go to the bathroom. It hurt to walk. I was dismayed to find drops of blood. Not a lot, but enough to know that something had torn. Our oldest son was nearing age 15 by then so he stayed with the other children while hubby took me to the hospital.

The new sonogram revealed that the babies were fraternal twin boys, each with their own amniotic sac and placenta. One of the placentas had become partially ripped from the uterine wall. I was admitted into the hospital for observation. We decided to name the boys Richard after my dad and David after my husband's favorite uncle who had drowned.

I lost Richard in the wee hours of the morning. He had died in my womb. I held off my grief because I put all of my energy into helping David stay alive. The doctor said that the trauma of birthing Richard didn't seem to cause a critical situation for David so it looked like we would have six children after all.

We were doing so much better that the doctor released me from the hospital on the afternoon of Christmas Eve so I could spend it with our family. I had strict orders to stay on the couch including nighttime sleeping and only get up to go to the bathroom, which was only about 15 feet away. My family was to do ALL the cooking, cleaning, laundry, and more. I was to be treated like a Queen!

The women at church organized meals to be brought over every day for at least a week, maybe longer, so I could get my strength back and David could grow.

We had a wonderful Christmas, focusing on the joy of the season and the increasing health of David, rather than focusing on the loss of Richard. It was only during the quiet hours in the middle of the night that I would let some tears fall.

In the morning, two days after Christmas I woke up to major cramping and a slow trickle of blood. Again, I was whisked to the hospital. The following day, which was also our second son's 13th birthday, I lost David.

Holding him in my hands for a few tearful moments, I called the nurse. I sobbed uncontrollably and evidently, I passed out. I vaguely remember being pushed through the halls on a gurney, periodically looking up at the blue-masked faces around me. I went in and out of consciousness.

I was hemorrhaging and they wanted to do an endometrium oblation (burn out the lining of my uterus). The medical personnel were explaining things to my husband to get permission, but I had an overwhelming feeling that I would be okay and that there was still another child in heaven who was waiting to be in our family.

God gave me the strength to deny permission and the bleeding stopped on its own. After a couple of days in the hospital, I returned home to start my healing journey. I am very grateful I was able to speak up and refuse the medical procedure which would have made another pregnancy impossible. Nine years after our fifth child, I gave birth to our sixth, a beautiful, healthy daughter. Although there are 19 years between the first and last, our family is complete.

I have learned some important things through my miscarriages and that healing is a deeply personal journey that can only be traveled by the one walking the path; no one else can define what that process looks like. It also can't be rushed. Ultimately, I had to follow my own heart. Looking back, I see that the grief came in waves; I was fine one minute and bawling my eyes out the next and that was okay.

I learned to forgive rather than blame and that not only meant other people who stressed me out or otherwise harmed me, but also myself. The miscarriages happened. It helped tremendously when I accepted them, surrendered my pain to God, and let it go without placing fault or playing the "if only" game.

I also learned to forgive people who said blunt, hurtful things unintentionally when I miscarried. Especially if they hadn't experienced it themselves, comments such as "at least it's better than losing a live baby" seemed heartless, but most likely people were sincerely trying to comfort me. Frankly, I think a lot of people just didn't know what to say.

I learned to be grateful for what I had but also not feel guilty for wanting more including the size of my family. Humans, as Children of God, are meant to grow and expand. We weren't meant to stay status quo.

I learned the importance of getting support. For me, it included close friends and family, health professionals, and clergy. There were also hot lines I could have used if I didn't have my own tribe already established.

I chose people who would listen with compassion but not feed into a victim mentality. If I chose to see myself as a victim, the pain would stay real and raw. I consciously embraced my pain and felt it to my core.

Another aspect of that was learning not to compare my grief with others. At first, I had thoughts tumble around in my head such as "I shouldn't hang on to this sorrow because so-and-so has it so much worse." The pain and sadness were real. I had to acknowledge it. I needed to feel it deeply and intensely before it could wash through me and clear out my heartache. This was when I could finally release it to God and let the healing began.

I was grateful to get away for a few days with my hubby during this grieving process. I needed the break from routine. It helped me regain my perspective and appreciate all the good in my life. It helped to reconnect and renew our relationship. We were able to talk, share, grieve and then heal together.

On the flip side of that, I also needed some time to be alone; to meditate, pray, cry, scream, and exercise, journal, dance... whatever it took to let the grief flow through me so I could release it. I then repeated as necessary. It was NOT an overnight process.

And lastly, I explored and nurtured what gives me joy. Besides being a fully present and fun mama, I returned to writing, which I had put off for years. Even now, I am constantly taking classes and webinars on a variety of subjects because I love to explore new things. My passions are to learn, grow, connect, and serve.

We are all on our own personalized journey. There is no right or wrong way to heal. And what works one day may not work the next. It is a process. Even after 20+ years, I still sometimes cry over the sons we lost. I don't know that I'll ever completely get over it but it doesn't stop me from fulfilling my goals and dreams.

If anyone invites me to a Pity Party, I politely decline. Life is too short to stay stuck in the muck.

Laura Susanne (Stewart) Shortridge, A little woman with a big heart grew up in Denton, TX, USA and still considers herself a "forever" Texan. A teen bride, she and her husband have been married over 40 years and have 3 sons, 3 daughters, and 3 grandchildren. She and her husband currently reside in gorgeous western New York state.

Laura believes in having multiple streams of income. She has multiple online businesses and owns a real estate investment company, but her favorite source of revenue comes from what she calls "word weaving."

As a woman of faith, Laura believes in helping others. That includes tithing to her church and supporting numerous individuals and nonprofit organizations that offer a hand up (not just a hand-out). She also loves to support other Dream-builders with projects that bring light to others.

Her passion at this time is to help individuals realize their true, divine worth and develop the God-given gifts placed in their hearts. Through her creative works, speaking engagements, and coaching, she hopes to make a positive impact on those in her sphere of influence.

To learn more about Laura, please visit her online at laurastewartshortridge.com.

Moving Beyond the Inner Pain: Becoming Stronger, Happier, and Healthier

Dorota Soto

It's June 2008 and I am rushing to pack all my summer clothes for my first ever trip to the U.S.A. Growing up in Poland my biggest dream was always to travel the world. And NYC was always on the top of my places to visit.

My dream is about to finally come true. I am excited yet anxious. I have never gone away by myself, for so long and so far away! But you live only once, right? I am 21 years old; summer vacation is about to start, and I am going to make the best out of it. Summer students exchange programs in Europe make it pretty easy for college kids to take on the adventure like this.

Arriving to the airport went smoothly. After settling down in the plane for the longest flight in my life, I plug in my earphones to my phone and being my journey that was to change my life forever.

JFK airport ended being overwhelmingly busy. But I can spot someone waving the name of the program on a big board. Ok, I think, I am safe! The next step is to get to the place where I am supposed to work for the entire summer. It is a hotel in a small Island on the very tip of Long Island NY called Shelter Island. My heart is beating from excitement and nervousness that accompanying this journey. I know no-one here; I am so far away from my family and friends. What have I been thinking? Luckily the girl who picked up the phone in the hotel, when I called to ask for a ride from the ferry, is Polish. What a relief. What can I say?

As the days went on it was the best summer I have ever had in my entire life. Working in the restaurant in one of the fanciest hotels so close to NYC seems so cool! I am having the time of my life with amazing people I work with, from all over the world. But most importantly I met a guy who I become to fall for deeply. The whole summer we are pretty much inseparable. He is 10 years older than me, and I know he is not just looking for a summer love. My mind and heart is spinning thinking about what will happen after the time to go back will come…

Summer is over. I can't stop crying. The only thing I want to do is to stay here, forever. But I'm trying to make an adult decision. I am going back to Poland; I will finish last eight months of my college and I will then move to NYC.

In June 2009 it is time for me to make a move across the Atlantic. I made a decision to be with him, and I am going to stick with my commitment even though I am terrified. Months later, on August 3rd. we are getting married! I am 22 and I am living a fun young girl lifestyle, working in restaurants and bars around NYC. My life mostly consists of late nights, partying, eating fast food and drinking. I mean a lot! I gained so much weight since moving here and I am slowly becoming very uncomfortable with my body and my lifestyle.

A few years later I am ready to make a change. I can't continue to go on like this. I always wanted to have kids one day and a respectful job (even though I have no idea what that even means). My interest in exercise and healthy eating is growing. And all of this sparks the passion in me for fitness and nutrition. And then it hit me…I'm going to get certified and become a personal trainer and nutrition coach. Boom! At this point in my life husband are not in the same place and we are slowly going in totally different directions.

During our whole relationship I was always made to believe that I am no one without him. I was very much dependent on him and I was convinced I am not worthy and capable of taking care of myself and/or create a success in my life. Finally, in 2013 we got divorced.

It is not a pretty one. I need to find to place to live, otherwise I will need to go back home. It is a very hard time for me. I still don't really have a lot of friends here or family. I have no savings at all. And I have no place to stay. And I am concerned that I am not capable enough of making it in foreign country on my own. Again, the thought returned that I need to go back to Poland. One of my personal training clients who also is my friend tells me that I have to stay and give it try and that I can totally make it here. So here it is. I am going to rent a room in Queens, and I am now determined to make things work for me.

I am really motivated to make this whole fitness work. I am still working behind the bar to be able to pay for my room and I am also working at the gym to try to build my business. All of the stress made me lose a lot of weight. I barely eat and I am in the obsessive workout mode, because I feel like this is the only thing that keeps me going and keeps me sane.

A few months later I met my current husband, Herman. He is the person who puts a smile on my face, helps me with all my insecurities and limiting beliefs and teaches me how to believe in myself. It's a 360 degree change from my previous relationship. Everything slowly is becoming better and more stable in my life. Life is good again. But on the other hand, I am struggling to find my balance. I go from obsessive dieting and working out like crazy to a period where I simply do not care at all.

I have that vision in my head that since I'm a trainer and nutrition coach I should be better. I am the person who should have this all figured out for myself. But it is not as easy as one would think. And I really struggle with this part which put more stress on me…

In April 2016 Herman a I get married! And we decided to buy a house! Everything is looking really good for us. Life is good. I am happy. I feel fulfilled.

I always wanted to have big family, and I know Herman is the person I want to have this with. Unfortunately, after being 20 weeks pregnant, during the anatomy scan we hear devastating news, we encounter major complications, and the baby won't make it. After that I am devastated, I feel like the whole world just collapsed on me. I am finding myself in some kind of self-destructive mode. I am drinking and eating more than usual and while I gained 10lbs during my short pregnancy it doesn't look like I'm going to lose any of it after losing the baby.

I hate my body. It feels foreign to me. It's a really a terrible place to be. It feels like the only place you should feel safe in, is not my place anymore. And there is no running away from it.

This becomes my turning point. I realize now firsthand that women can go through so many different stages and experiences in the life that can reshape their life going forward. In a few months I decide it's time to move forward with my life.

I start my journey of self-development. I went through internal shifts that caused external shifts. Yes, I lost weight but the most important thing is that I now finally feel comfortable in my body for the first time in my life. It was hard and challenging work, but I am coming out on the other side stronger than before. I know many women suffer in silence and long to know they are not walking this path alone. As much as I would never wish anyone going through this experience, for me knowing that there are other women who are here to support you, was and still is a huge step in my recovery! This adversity taught me that I am stronger and more resilient than I ever could have imagined.

Feeling worthy is my birth right. Even though I have amazing support around me in friends, family and my amazing husband, I now can call myself with full belief an independent woman.

All my life experiences transformed my life. I have big dreams and I am not afraid to go after them. I have a vision and mission for my life. I lean more into my spirituality which further fuels my drive to live my life with a purpose. Daily yoga, meditation, journaling, and exercise is my ultimate recipe for overcoming hard moments and setbacks in my life. And daily gratitude practice! After adversity, it's challenging to be in the present moment and feel grateful for all that I have. But practicing gratitude helps to widen my perspective and look at things more broadly, increases my positivity and well-being, and improves my confidence and relationships with others. At times like these, when things are not going the way I want them to, a gratitude practice can be a stabilizer. I am committed to practicing self-love to nourishing the most important relationship I have in my live: the one with myself. It is my understanding that I don't need validation from external sources, but I am already perfect just as I am.

And until I found this space of peace and acceptance within, I was always looking elsewhere. Which explains my unsuccessful relationship where I let the other person dictate who I should be and what I should do with my life. A grateful heart is a magnet for miracles. Once I started to live a life from a place of gratitude for all I have rather than from a place of scarcity, my attitude towards life, myself, and ultimately, how I love and accept myself totally changed. I journal every day, and one part of it is writing things I am grateful for! This practice truly changed my life!

The moment I realized I am healing was the moment I felt hopeful again. I am no longer crying every single day and I take things into my hands to get out of the darkest moments. I feel happy again and excited about my life. Also being busy helps. From my experience sitting down only triggers more unwanted thoughts and emotions. When I was grieving, my manager at work offered to give me extra time off but I declined. I needed to go back to work, to my regular life as soon as possible. On top of it mine and my husband's focus on "getting back in shape" was a huge distraction that takes my attention away from my experience. Now I plan more fun events with friends, and every day I work on building my independent personal training and nutrition coaching business which is definitely a huge distraction! And a great help!

People don't like to talk about the darkest moments of their lives. But my personal experience taught me that knowing that there are others walking the same path can be very helpful. And hearing a success stories of women who experiences the loss of a baby, gave me so much hope. And that's why I am so inspired to share my story. I hope it will help someone else to heal as well!

My inner pain transformed me into more compassionate person. It brought a different perspective into my life and my coaching business. Now I am grateful for all that it was and for all that is beyond measures and I know there is still so much more that awaits me!

Dorota Soto is a personal trainer and nutritionist. Originally from Poland but she's been living in the USA since 2009.

Her journey with wellness began 8 years ago when she fell in love with all things fitness and decided to help others create a more active lifestyle.

Throughout all these years she struggled with finding balance in her life that works for her, constant dieting, and excessive exercising. And even when she was in a "good" place, she might have looked fit on the outside but her mind was not, constantly beating herself up for not being good enough.

After her miscarriage in 2019 Dorota found herself in self destructive mode. After two months of grieving she decided it's time to move forward with her life. She started her journey of self-development.

Dorota went through an internal shift that caused an external shift. She lost weight but most importantly she finally started to feel comfortable in her body for the first time in her life.

Dorota's mission is to help women create powerful relationships with their body so they can feel comfortable in their own skin. Her approach to weight loss is different because she believes that life lasting transformation starts in your mind.

Dorota works hard to deliver the best results to her clients. She's proudly certified Personal Trainer through NSC, Master Nutrition Coach through Precision Nutrition Level 1 & 2, Pre and Post Natale Coach through Girls Gone Strong and Online Trainer through Online Trainer Academy

To learn more about Dorota, please visit her website at dorotasoto.com.

Anxiety Diary: A Journey to Self-Discovery

Carrie Thompson

Have you ever felt alone, misunderstood, unworthy and broken? I experienced those feelings for most of my life but never more than when I was diagnosed with generalized anxiety disorder (GAD). I knew I was an incessant worrier that frequently played out the worst case scenarios for everything in my life, but I never realized that I had a mental health disorder.

I am 34 years old and back when I was growing up, no one talked about mental health or mental health disorders. If they did, it was always "something is just not right with that person." I thought of mental health disorders as the extreme cases of schizophrenia and other chronic afflictions with traits that present more obvious to outsiders, not anxiety, depression or PTSD, because that was all I saw on television or in movies. I think the misconceptions and stigmas around mental health and mental health disorders set me up for failure as an adult, because when I got my diagnosis, it felt like a death sentence.

In elementary school I was bullied for being overweight. While I may have been a fun, friendly, talented and intelligent child, this overshadowed everything. It was bad enough that all of my friends were thin and cute, because I was always comparing myself, but then to have people point it out to me specifically really messed me up.

I will never forget the time my neighbor compared my size to the Titanic ship. I was still in elementary school and he announced it loudly on the bus. I was mortified. I knew I was overweight, but that was so embarrassing. This was the true beginning of my low self-esteem, low self-worth and confidence and would continue on through my 20's.

As time went on, more factors fed into my insecurity. From a fairly young age, I compared myself to my friends. They were good at anything they set out to do...school work, singing, musical instruments, etc. They were also very sweet and beautiful, popular among most other kids at school. They were all in the gifted program at school, so they were taken out of class and put into a special program at times due to their level of intelligence. They were nominated for homecoming, high school superlatives, leadership roles, you name it. Compared to them, I felt rejected, and at times, invisible.

My insecurity grew with each school year. I was sick of being the fat girl and the summer after freshman year of high school, I decided to do something about it. It started with daily trips to the YMCA for a workout. While this seems like a harmless and positive life change, I took it to the extreme. I was in there every day for hours. If I didn't get in my workout, I freaked out and was in the worst mood. I also started developing an eating disorder. Within the first month, I was an anorexic.

I lost about 70 pounds. You would think I would be happy with my new body and excited to show it off. Nope. When you develop an eating disorder and an addiction to exercise, you also develop extreme body dysmorphia and a lot of mental health issues. No matter how thin I became, I felt I would be happier if I lost two more pounds. If I lost two more pounds, then I wanted to lose two more. It was addictive. This cycle continued on for a long time. Eventually, I started eating more because the anorexia was destroying my body and leaving me exhausted. However, the exercise addiction continued on well into my 30's.

In addition to my body image issues, I felt like I had to overcompensate for what I lacked in every area of life. This overcompensation led to attention-seeking and obnoxious behavior. I was loud, boisterous, and at times, mean. My insecurity led me to abandon my incredible childhood friends and connect with all of the wrong kinds of people, consequently ruining my senior year of high school. Where I should have been celebrating my successes with my girlfriends, I was putting myself in risky situations just so these new "friends" would like me.

As I entered college, my insecurity led to more attention-seeking behavior; dressing and dancing sexy in the clubs, drinking too much, promiscuous behavior, and skipping class. And let's not forget, the incessant working out. I'm thankful for my terrible body dysmorphia only because it allowed me to meet one of my best friends in the entire world, but three hours a day at the gym paired with college drinking and eating habits destroyed my metabolism.

By the grace of God, I earned my bachelor's degree in December of 2009 in Strategic Communications and a minor in Sociology. I loved every moment of my college years and wish I could relive them with the knowledge I have now, but by the time I graduated, it was time to grow up. I didn't think I would ever accomplish my professional goals if I stayed in Columbus (Go Buckeyes!), because I was so comfortable in my service industry and party lifestyle, so I uprooted myself and moved to North Carolina.

In August 2010, I moved down south with hopes of starting a new life. Unfortunately, due to the financial crisis and resulting job market, I fell back into my old ways. I was bartending and partying it up with all of my new friends, not making one step forward on the career path of my dreams. While bartending, I had a short stint as a bank teller, another as a recruiter and finally a marketing role that turned into me being the office errand girl. I hated them all.

In that final role, I was talked down to because I was a woman, as were the other two female employees. We were spoken to and treated as if we were stupid just because of our gender. It made me so mad. I knew I was more intelligent than half the men in there and if I was just allowed to shine, I would do great things. This anger was the great awakening I needed. I prayed God would send me the answer and that materialized in the grand idea of going to grad school.

In preparation to quit that awful administrative job, I began to study for the GMAT. This time around, I was determined to choose a career path with job stability. I landed on accounting. A few of my family members were already accountants and my parents had technical jobs. I just felt it was meant to be. After passing the GMAT with flying colors, I applied to Winthrop University's graduate school accounting program and got in. I was so excited for this next step on my journey.

Because my degree was in the arts, I had to complete all the undergraduate accounting course work before I could start my grad classes. After my first class, I knew I had made the right decision. Accounting came easily to me, and I felt so productive being back in school. I cruised through grad school with ease, staying more focused and studying instead of partying. The only hurdle I had to overcome was the CPA exam, which consists of four separate exams. In order to pass, you had to pass all four exams, with a score of 75 or greater, all within an 18 month window. Once completed, you would be deemed a certified public accountant.

I knew I was going to take the exam as soon as I entered the accounting program. It isn't required in order to find a job, but makes you stand out from other candidates and qualifies you for higher paying roles. As soon as I graduated, I started studying and made it my full-time job. I only worked weekends and spent 8+ hours a day in my dad's office watching study prep videos and completing practice questions. I was determined to get 100% on all four parts, which was extremely unrealistic, so naturally this took a dark turn. My perfectionist tendencies were about to catch up to me.

By the time I finished the second exam, I started to have panic attacks in the middle of the night. The first time it happened, I had no clue what was going on and thought I was having a heart attack. Naturally, I hit up Dr. Google and tried every at-home remedy the web suggested, including jumping into a freezing cold shower, to stop my "heart attack." This continued on for months, with numerous trips to the emergency room. This was when my mental health issues truly became apparent.

Obviously, my mental health issues started much younger, but I had no clue they afflicted me back then. I didn't realize the eating disorder, body dysmorphia, catastrophizing and constant worry were causes for concern. It wasn't until my mental health started affecting my physical health that I acknowledged its existence and sought help.

After numerous panic attacks, nights without sleep and tear-filled study sessions, I was diagnosed with generalized anxiety disorder. Eventually, my general practitioner gave me Xanax and recommended starting Zoloft. I thought these medications were going to be the miracle fix I needed to get back to my "normal" self. That is not the case at all. Not educating myself prior to beginning these medications was a huge mistake. I thought anxiety medication was just like taking Tylenol. Take a pill, wait 30 minutes, feel much better. That is certainly not how it works and no one warned me.

The Xanax worked fine for me and did its job to calm me down during moments of complete panic. The Zoloft, however, had greater consequences. Everything was fine for a few days, but once I started increasing the dosage, per my GP's instruction, I felt worse than I had before. This eventually led to suicidal ideation, which was the most terrifying moment of my life. I'll never forget it; I had just gotten out of the shower and was standing in my bedroom getting ready for the day. Out of nowhere, this horrible feeling came over me and I collapsed on my bed crying. As the minutes ticked by, it got worse. I knew that I had to get dressed as fast as possible and race to my parent's house.

The entire drive to my parents' house I was battling with my own mind. "You do not want to kill yourself. These feelings aren't real. You are going to be ok." As soon as I arrived, I broke down in my mom's arms. The next day, I was instructed to immediately stop taking the medication and was informed that around 1% of people have that reaction to antidepressants. Lucky me.

After I stopped the medication it took over a month to feel better. During that time, I was instructed to live with my parents while I got back on my feet. I stopped studying and some days could do little more than go on a walk with mom or dad. While my brain fought through this recovery process, we decided that I should find a therapist to try to heal holistically. My mom did extensive research to find someone accredited and suitable. After days of hunting she scheduled an appointment. I was nervous to go and felt such a deep sense of embarrassment that things had gotten this bad. But I really had nothing to fear. By the grace of God, my mom had somewhat randomly chosen the person who would become my lifeline over the following few years.

Ashley was a gem. She was kind, understanding, relatable, supportive you name it. I wondered why I didn't talk to a therapist earlier because if this is how all therapists were then what was I so afraid of. We were perfectly compatible, which I would not fully appreciate until I crawled back to her years later. She knew how to challenge and push me when I was being resistant or lazy, where other therapists I had seen during a period of her absence took a more relaxed approach. She was quick-witted and intelligent, soaking up everything I said and almost never forgetting a single detail. She was just what I didn't know I needed.

Unfortunately, I thought therapy would be another miracle fix, just like I assumed the medication would remedy all my problems, which meant I tended to be lazy. If something didn't work on the first try, I gave up. I wasn't 100% comfortable with her right off the bat, because therapy is just like any relationship and takes time, so I wasn't always honest or forthcoming with information. Once I was feeling more like myself and didn't feel like going because I wanted to go out with friends or something, I would cancel. So while Ashley was doing all she could, I was only putting in 50% effort and eventually stopped going all together.

I think we all fall into this trap at some point in our lives. When shit gets tough, we search endlessly for a quick fix, because humans hate discomfort. We stumble upon a few options, some good and some bad...medication, therapy, exercise, diets, alcohol or drug abuse, etc., but once life improves and we feel like ourselves again, we stop trying or end up with bigger problems than we started with. I've been guilty of this more than a few times during my life and it took a while to finally recognize the error of my ways. That did not happen during this time frame. It took a few more years of toxic behavior, moments of crisis and even a full mental breakdown, which sent me back to my parents' house for three months, to finally open my eyes.

We know the old saying "anything worth having isn't easy" We may think that's a cliché, but it's actually a fact. If I would have educated myself on my treatment options when I first got diagnosed with generalized anxiety disorder, including finding a psychiatrist, maybe my medication experience wouldn't have been so terrible. Five years later, I am on Paxil and Lamictal and have never felt better. I found myself a psychiatrist and asked lots of questions before popping a pill this time, which I assure you wasn't easy. I was traumatized after that first experience, but I'm glad I went to an expert and took their advice.

I am back in therapy full-time and have been for over two years. I'm still with Ashley, because luckily she took me back after all my nonsense. The first year or so, I didn't really give it my all. I will openly admit that. I was full of excuses as to why I wasn't getting better or why I couldn't do what she was asking or bullshit reasons why what she said didn't apply to me. It took my mental breakdown for me to finally get my act together and do the work. The really hard work.

She had always told me "you won't do the work until you reach your breaking point and don't have another choice." She was right.

Most importantly, I work on myself now because I want to. I have implemented more positive habits in my personal life. I take the exercises we discuss in therapy and try to practice them every day. I try to focus on gratitude and actively work to turn my catastrophic thoughts down a more optimistic path. I stopped relying on alcohol. I still get drinks with friends or have a glass of wine with dinner, but definitely have more self-control than in the past. This has been a game changer for my anxiety. I also cut all toxic and unsupportive individuals out of my life.

None of this is easy. Sometimes I spiral and the shit gets dark. Instead of beating myself up about it, I remind myself that EVERYONE has bad days. Then I just deal with my bad day, going to bed hopeful for a brighter day tomorrow. I use movement as medicine on a daily basis. Getting the blood pumping is a great way to boost endorphins and a positive outlet for any negative energy you're carrying. I surround myself with kind, positive, loving, caring, supportive, inclusive individuals who work hard and live the same values as myself. I have started setting more goals so that I never become stagnant and continually educate and improve myself. All of this has made a world of difference.

I needed a little bit of encouragement. I wasn't perfect and I needed to stop trying to be. I realize that society set me up for unrealistic standards in the way of trying to be like everyone else and I fell for it. It wasn't until I looked inward and examined my own life and what I wanted to change that I finally took the steps I needed to heal. It was when I acknowledged what I was most proud of that I saw the path forward.

My biggest goal right now is to be a voice for others who have gone through what I have, to raise awareness for the importance of mental health, and to be an example of what a little bit of hard work can do.

Carrie Thompson is a CPA, Mental Health Advocate, the Author of *Anxiety Diary of an Ordinary Girl,* and co-author of the anthology, *Embracing the Journey: Inspiring Stories of Hope, Healing and Triumphing over Adversity.*

Diagnosed with generalized anxiety disorder (GAD) in 2016, Carrie spent time exploring the world of mental health and educating herself on the causes and the cures. She is passionate about helping others and aspires to change lives by bringing awareness to the importance of mental health through sharing her story, expanding others' knowledge, and connecting with them.

FOX, NBC, and CBS have featured Carrie, and she has contributed to Thrive Global, and various other websites, digital magazines, and podcasts have interviewed her.

In addition to reading and writing, she enjoys fitness and baking. She loves to spend time with her family, friends, and sweet kitty, Albie.

To learn more about Carrie, please visit her website at alwaysgrowingwithgratitude.com.

Transformation of Self: Turning Wounds into Wisdom Through Healing My Identity

Esmeralda Tridevi

Have you ever heard that old expression, what doesn't kill you, will make you stronger? Well, if that quote was personified, it would be my life! The first time I heard that saying, I was no older than eight. I read it off one of my moms' old tee-shirts. I would always over analyze it, never quite understanding how crucial it was to one's personal development. At the time, I am only subconsciously aware of the everlasting cycle of the healing process. My identity has always felt slightly distorted but here I stand strong, in my effort to heal all parts of me.

I am what I am: a spiritual teacher, a caretaker, a provider, a storyteller, a lover, a healer, an artist, a medicine muse, and a Goddess.

Very early in my life, by the age of 10, I knew that pain was a feeling that was deeper than physical wounds. I was aware of those lower frequency states of being such as regret, jealousy, guilt, denial, and anger. I witnessed the heaviness of grief and how it could engulf you. Fear is another one of those feelings that kept me paralyzed, struggling to make sense of life. Unable to make any moves. It's like being smothered by a wet weighted blanket. I only had seen it in proximity; never up close and personal.

Throughout my early adolescence and teenage years, I questioned everything around me. To this day, I still consider myself to be a more existential person. I still wonder the meaning of life and what my purpose here truly is.

Ask my mother, she would tell you my favorite question is WHY? Why this? Why that? Why did this happen? Why do I have to do this? Why am I here? I always laugh when I think back to my school days. I was completely uninterested in the teachings, nor did I feel I resonated with my classmates at all. Even now, I am healing the wound that still gets irritated whenever I am being told what to do by an authority I do not trust. There was always the underlying knowing that what I was being taught was not the curriculum that was ultimately important for my growth and expansion.

The only lessons that piqued my interest was that of the creative arts. My favorite form of expression is speaking, singing, and writing. Whether it's poetry, wanting to write a full book, or sharing a song, it will always be a form of meditation for me. My throat chakra, which houses communication, truthfulness, and creativity, was closed for a long time. I suppressed my beautiful expressions for too long and let me just say, it feels damn good to be writing right now.

I had lots of angry outbursts throughout my teenage years. I had a lot of built-up resentment from me not having a relationship with my father. Bless my mother for raising me all on her own. My mind was met with puzzling confusion because I didn't understand why my family seemed so broken and detached. I am still piecing that puzzle together. Religion has been a big divider. What happened to our bloodline? I'm very curious, particularly the bloodline of the women in our family. There is, however, much more acceptance of how my family chooses to live their life, and if a few words could sum up how it is, it would be isolated in fantasy. I recognize one of the great challenges for me in this life is that of forgiveness. Live and Let Live.

Over the years I have learned how to deeply relax my temper. The biggest stress relievers for me are sacred plant medicine, Yoga, dance, singing, and later, after going deeper into the studies of how we can heal ourselves, using the power of meditational breathing.

I was 10 years old and very eager to write about my experiences of where I was living at the time. I wrote about a traumatic experience in which I saw the aftermath of a young woman who had injured her own wrists, she laid there, seemingly unconscious. My mother and I helped her as much as possible. I remember feeling this unique balance of empathy, understanding, but also confusion as to why it happened. This profoundly visual moment opened all three of my eyes very early in life.

Presently, I spend my days offering intuitive energy medicine work. When I feel inspired to create impact through my community, I share my loving energy at special events and sacred gatherings where respect, love, and honor radiates all around. I love creating and sharing soulfully rich art that inspires people to live more freely. Whether I am healing though my hands on energy work or just by holding loving space, people benefit greatly from working with me because I can put myself in their shoes and truly help solve the problems they are facing.

I have been on my conscious soul healing journey now for about five years. I had a spontaneous Kundalini awakening that left me shook to my core when I was around 20 years old. My stability was gone. My connection to all that is, was severed. I felt a complete lack of love because I did not know how to love or honor myself. I understand now, that one of the best ways for me to show myself love, is by listening and following my intuition. Currently, I am so deep down the spiritual rabbit hole, I've become like Alice in Wonderland, but it took years to discover this magickal place. Life was not always this colorful and wonderous.

There are so many factors that play into why I felt so alone and suppressed throughout my life, but I feel there is one moment above the rest that changed my life forever. I witnessed and experienced a lot of traumatizing events. Most of them are surrounding relationships, depression, anger, and addiction which I have suffered from personally and am still healing. All of these being the utmost triggering for me. The most triggering and truthfully karmic lesson is what we call death.

The year was 2016. I had just started massage therapy school. Everything in my life was going seemingly well; aside from the part where I discovered that my romantic partner had been addicted to hard drugs for years. I was clueless. This deep reality shaped my outlook on life into one that was very dramatic and confusing. The world around me was chaotic and uncertain. The deep truth is that my inner-world, full of trapped painful thoughts, and feelings unexpressed, is what was keeping me feeling stuck for such a long time. We had a very intense relationship that is now very hard to remember and even harder to forget. We were twin flames that would have eventually burnt down everything around us, in the name of love.

What is death? Isn't that one of the great mysteries? In my opinion, death is not the end of our existence. It is the end of our time here physically, in this human avatar, living out this simulation of reality. Death is such a scary word. I often wondered why we even keep track of time. What is time? It must've been because we wanted to keep track of our mortality.

February 6th, 2017, I lost my dear beloved due to a drug overdose, 2 weeks before her 21st birthday. We were together on and off for a few years before our tumultuous relationship came to a crashing halt. Even now, 5 years later, I still cry when I think about the harsh reality of what happened. I was on my way to work when I received a dreadful message in text. I immediately rushed into full rage mode and drove as fast as I could, heart racing, eyes bloodshot red, all the way to her house. There I met the family and cried until my tears were all dried up and stuck to my face and there was nothing left to say. There were so many questions that I had, but I didn't feel it was even appropriate to ask. But the one thing I was certain of was that I was madly in love with a person who could barely love themself and that was on me.

I had to teach myself to purposefully block out the memory of our fights, and trust me, they got bad. The imagery that comes up for me now, is a picture of two hands. One hand is holding on tightly to a rope, the hand very tense and obviously in pain. The other hand was spread wide open, and you see the same rope being freed from the painful grip. There is an illustration that says something like "sometimes holding on hurts worse than just letting go."

I choose to remember her in the brightest light. I remember her as my best friend, the person who introduced me to psychedelics, and the person who introduced me to the EDM / Rave community. In a lot of ways, I credit who I am today, to the relationship we shared. I recognize and honor her as one of my strongest guardian angels and for this, I am eternally protected and blessed.

I honor you E.R, M.C, B.F, D.F, and T.B. I have shared unforgettable memories with you all. Thank you, beautiful souls for experiencing this life with me, with love. You all have transitioned peacefully past your human form, as I knew you. I now know you as the wind, the rain, the fire, and the earth. The music in my ears, and the flutter in my heart.

My heart has become completely cracked open. The first defining lesson in my transformation of self: It did not start with me, but it will end with me. "IT" being the trauma, the grief, pain, lack, or feelings of inadequacy and being unfulfilled. We are born into this world from our parents and sometimes it is the relationships and events from your parents' lives, and from your grand-parent's lives' etc. that can affect your upbringing.

The second concept that continues to help me process and balance my emotions is: there is no such thing as right and wrong. It is all a matter of choice. I chose, whether I realize it in the moment, to fulfil a soul contract with everyone I meet.

The bittersweet lesson whenever I start to feel defeated is that my healing never ends. I take each moment as it comes. I do not have to have it all figured out at once. It's like I am on one of those giant village wheels that cycle's water through the lake. It always feels like a wild ride. When listening closely, I hear the universe, asking me to hold on tight and just breathe while getting plunged into the ice-cold water. I often have these cycles of being on top, feeling victorious in this game of life and other times I feel dragged down to the bottom of the wheel, suffocating under so much pressure.

It truly is a vicious and beautiful cycle, because each time I get plunged into the water, I learn. I am taught how not to panic. I have patience, trust, and I know this is all part of my healing process.

Esmeralda Sierra Rainboe Tridevi is a sensual spirit life coach and intuitive activation healer who has a deep love for connecting with nature, taboo, the sensual arts, and all things spiritual.

She is one wild, wise soul!

Soon after graduating college in 2017 as a Massage Therapist, she knew traveling to share the healing arts was her soul's calling. This heart-centered warrioress fully activated her devotion to the healing path when she, later on, became an Usui Holy Fire Reiki Master Teacher in 2020.

Sierra believes everyone is deserving of an abundant soul-rich life. Her lifestyle of travel, performing arts, storytelling, nude modeling, and tantric practice moves to end suppression and sexual stigma around the way society views sensuality and to empower healing and transformation of their own traumas into wisdom and strength.

She often says it's the pressure that creates the crystal; strong, illuminating, and ever evolving.

To learn about 1:1 mentorships, classes, ceremonies, with Esmeralda, go explore her website at wildandwiseremedies.com.

www.ingramcontent.com/pod-product-compliance
Lightning Source LLC
Chambersburg PA
CBHW071546040426
42452CB00008B/1099